How to Be Normal

A Guide for the Perplexed

GUY BROWNING has made a career bringing profound thinking to places where it really isn't needed. He is the Creative Director of the innovation agency Smokehouse, a writer, film director and dad dancer. He lives in the Vale of the White Horse, Oxfordshire, England.

HOW TO BE NORMAL

A Guide for the Perplexed

Guy Browning

ATLANTIC BOOKS
LONDON

Published in Great Britain in 2014 by
Atlantic Books, an imprint of Atlantic Books Ltd.

This paperback edition published in Great Britain
in 2015 by Atlantic Books.

2 4 6 8 10 9 7 5 3 1

A CIP catalogue record for this book is available
from the British Library.

Paperback ISBN: 978 1 78239 584 3
E-book ISBN: 978 1 78239 583 6

Printed and bound in Great Britain by
Clays Ltd, St Ives plc

Atlantic Books
An imprint of Atlantic Books Ltd
Ormond House
26–27 Boswell Street
London WC1N 3JZ

www.atlantic-books.co.uk

This book is dedicated with love
to Ceci, Theo and Will.

My warmest thanks go to the professionals
behind this book: Margaret Stead, Toby Mundy,
Lauren Finger, Bunmi Oke, Richard Evans,
James Roxburgh, Ben Dupré, Juliet Mushens,
Sarah Manning and the incomparable
Janet Brown.

Contents

Contents

Rubbing Along

How to be Normal

Normal people are extremely unusual. Think of all the people you know and ask yourself how many are normal. None of them. In fact you're probably the most normal of the lot. Of course, normality is clearly a relative thing. If you have relatives, they're unlikely to be normal.

Normal people wear things that aren't trendy but neither are they uncool. Only when flared trousers hit the high street will normal people be wearing them. Abnormal people will have worn them willy-nilly for the last twenty years.

Normal people don't have their own taste in anything. They like whatever is good at the moment. Not really good but averagely good. The fashion industry is dedicated to changing what is normal. That's why models and what they wear never look normal.

Normal people don't ask you what you do for a living because this only encourages you to ask what they do and what they do is very normal. It's something so normal that conversations usually falter after they tell you. Normal people do normal things in bed with other normal people. Occasionally they try something a little bit different or they do it with somebody a little bit different. Again, all perfectly normal.

Normal people are distinguished by the fact that they all believe they are a little bit different, a little bit unique and a little bit special. This feeling is shared by all normal people. The only people who don't share this are wide-eyed staring eccentrics who think that they are perfectly normal.

Being normal is actually a very good disguise for being a barking eccentric. Under many a V-neck sweater there beats a heart of utter bizarreness. When multiple axe-murderers are discovered, the comments of the neighbours always tend to be along the lines of 'he seemed perfectly normal'.

Most normal people have something about themselves that they consider to be abnormal, like big ears, or no hair, or a funny voice, or pigeon toes. These people would rather that they had normal ears, hair, voice, toes, etc. But there's only one place on earth where people are perfectly normal and that's Hollywood. In our own minds we all have star potential if only Hollywood wasn't obsessed with hyper-normality.

It's actually very galling to know that everything you do in life is perfectly normal. Trying to do something interesting and different is a real challenge, but millions and millions of people are struggling to do it. There is in fact one thing that makes us all completely different, distinct and excitingly unique individuals, but you'll have to find that out for yourselves.

How to be Nice

In the fifties people used to aspire to nice things. With inflation, niceness is worth almost nothing and people now want incredible, sensational or awesome things. Enjoyment has been super-sized. There are few remaining things that people want to be nice – everyone wants a nice cup of tea but virtually no one wants nice sex.

Being nice hovers between being a virtue and a vice. Nice can be quite good but saying something is very nice is just a millimetre this side of bad. Not very nice at all is not at all nice. Saying 'Have a nice day' has never really caught on in this country. It's impossible to say it without giving the impression that what you really want that person to have is an absolute stinker of a day.

It's very difficult to put your finger on exactly what 'nice' means and that's why a biscuit has been specially designed to help. The Nice biscuit has a layer of sugar on the top to make it seem sweet, but essentially it's very dull. The same can be said of nice people.

Nice biscuits aren't sexy, which is why churches often

serve them with coffee. Nice people aren't sexy either. In fact there's an established grade of men in women's eyes. 'Sweet' means I like him but don't fancy him. 'Nice' means I don't fancy him or particularly like him. 'I really hate him' means I am in love with him.

In fact being nice is a lot like being a born-again Christian except without the Christianity or rebirth. What you're left with is an aggressive pleasantness and a willingness to make coffee at the drop of a hat (with Nice biscuits).

In general there are three vital elements of being nice. The first one is to give lifts to people even though they are going in the opposite direction. The second is to offer people tea and coffee immediately on meeting them. The third is to listen to people and nod. Really nice people can do all three things at once, which is why they always have a thermos in their car and are incredibly dangerous on the roads.

Nasty people often take advantage of nice people. However, it's the nasty people who end up getting hurt because they are then identified as people in need of niceness and will be harassed by kind people doing nice things for them twenty-four hours a day.

Interestingly, when two nice people get into a relationship, the niceness can suddenly go bad. It's almost impossible for two people to make tea for each other at once, with the result that you get crowding, confusion and resentment building up around the kettle area.

How to Understand

Understanding is something very few people really understand. Most people do overstanding, which is thinking you know about something without taking the trouble to find out about it. Beware of people who tell you they understand: it generally means they are tired of listening.

Living through something is the best way to understand it, but we can't live through everything so we have to listen to people who have. Amazingly, humans generally choose to learn the hard way rather than listen the easy way.

There's a Latin saying, *Ars longa, vita brevis*, which roughly translates as 'Life is short but understanding how to live takes a long time.' There's another similar phrase, *Dies longus, vitabix*, which means 'The day is long, have a good breakfast.' Both are worth remembering.

Understanding comes in four phases: ignorance, knowledge, experience, understanding. Both first and fourth phases are blissful, while the two intermediate ones are painful. Some people make the mistake of amassing knowledge and experience in spades without ever getting understanding. This has all the disadvantages of ignorance with none of the bliss.

Traditional cultures respect the elderly because of their greater understanding. Modern culture venerates youth and inexperience. Raising the retirement age is therefore a great way of reducing the average ignorance in the workplace.

Understanding is always provisional because it takes time and, more often than not, by the time you've understood something it's probably changed. Philosophers think you can understand things just by thinking about them. This works until you get hungry: no amount of thinking will help you understand a beef and ale pie.

Understanding yourself is hard work and many people prefer to get someone else to do it for them. If you go into therapy, remember that it's only successful when you come out. Therapy takes place on a couch, but it would be much quicker and cheaper if you had to hang from a bar and the session was over when you let go.

Understanding is not always a good thing; poetry, opera and sausage-making are all better for not being entirely understood. Similarly we wouldn't fall in love quite so fast if we understood the other person completely before we started. In general people don't like to be understood: it makes them feel like they've been completely consumed and only crumbs of interest are left.

How to be Moderate

Moderation in all things is good but you can overdo it. Often it is the most moderate politicians who are given to sexual and alcoholic excess in their private lives. Similarly, political extremists tend to be very moderate at home.

It's almost impossible to build a social or religious movement on moderation principally because moderation doesn't move forward, it budges up to accommodate. You'll notice that municipal statues are generally of people standing up pointing somewhere. You don't get statues of moderates sitting in their armchairs, listening intently and weighing up the pros and cons.

Moderation sounds rather genteel but is the hardest road to tread. Extremism has all the easy answers. For example it's very difficult to hold the position that global warming is happening only slightly and isn't apocalyptic. Light green is not a colour recognized by environmentalists. Similarly, the Church of England will be torn apart by its militant extremists unless its moderates decide to burn them all at the stake to calm them down.

The British are suspicious of extremists and are instinctively moderate. The fact that the custard cream is the nation's favourite biscuit tends to bear this out: it's a bland filling held between two tasteless biscuits. Indeed, that almost perfectly describes our political set-up as well.

Moderators are people who chair Presbyterian meetings or groups on the internet. Group moderators on the net are faceless people of probity, intelligence and great judgement. It's a shame they can't wear some sort of medal in public so we might know who these digital Solomons are. But then modesty is the handmaiden of moderation.

Moderation can be very dangerous, especially when you're trying to do something difficult and extreme. For example, bungee jumping off the kitchen table is likely to be far more dangerous than doing it off the Humber Bridge.

It's not a good idea to fall moderately in love and is in fact mildly insulting to the object of your lukewarm affection. A moderate lover would sign their Valentine cards 'Yours sincerely' and send bunches of watercress instead of red roses. They wouldn't fall in love either, they would step gingerly into love. Love is an extreme, which is why it's strangely unnerving watching Liberal Democrats mate.

How to Smile

Humans are the only species that smiles. Other animals may smile but it's probably behind our backs. A smile is the sunroof of the head (although in a slightly different position). It lets the sunshine in your soul pour through for a moment until you revert to normal overcast conditions.

Smiles come with teeth or without. A smile without teeth is a grin and this is often preferred by people with bad teeth. One of the reasons Americans can seem overly jolly is because they all have good teeth and don't mind displaying them. British teeth have been rotten for centuries and, as a smile was often like lifting a drain cover, we developed a stiff upper lip instead.

The ability to smile under pressure is hugely valuable: it's impossible to be intimidated, patronized, insulted or religiously converted when you're smiling. People like smiles but they're also suspicious of them. Unless the cause of your merriment is obvious, people will assume you're smiling at some deficiency on their part.

Smiles are incredibly fragile things. They're little bubbles of happiness and confidence that have managed to surface through the layers of angst, oppression and general misery. Incredibly, there are people who like nothing better than wiping the smile from people's faces. These people are the confiscators of life's footballs.

The ability of two people to smile continuously into each other's eyes is reserved for lovers and for mothers and their babies. Given this fact, a smile could easily be classified as a reproductive organ. Indeed, some cultures require that an erect smile be covered with the hand or a veil.

Real smiles involve the eyes. Customer-service people can arrange their teeth into a smile but have trouble getting their eyes to co-ordinate. Raised eyebrows are a sure sign of a genuine smile as it's incredibly difficult to do anything mean-spirited when they're in this position.

Clever people rarely smile. They know that village idiots smile at the slightest thing and they don't want to be mistaken for people concerned with slight things. Ironically, a smile can achieve things any amount of cleverness can't.

Smiles are like coal; using either contributes to global warming. Smiles are sometimes equally difficult to dig up. When you're feeling glum, you can jump-start happiness by smiling artificially. This reminds you how to do it and also feels so foolish you might smile despite yourself.

How to be Spontaneous

It's generally accepted that life is not a rehearsal. This may explain why a lot of people seem to be making a total hash of it – because they haven't rehearsed and they're just making things up as they go along. Spontaneous reaction to life can be viewed positively or negatively. One man's glorious devil-may-care spontaneity is another woman's panicking headless chicken.

Being spontaneous when you're talking is a matter of always saying the first thing that comes into your head. It's a technique that's been perfected in Yorkshire. There it's called straight talking and is often followed by a straight smack in the mouth.

British culture is based firmly on the suppression of spontaneity. What we do exceedingly well is ceremonial, which is at the other end of the spectrum. You'll wait a long time before you see a spontaneous Trooping the Colour. There are certain areas where spontaneity is particularly dangerous. Returning a work email with your first furious reaction is one of them and is the office equivalent of Tourette's syndrome.

Genuine acts of spontaneity need a great deal of planning. For example, if you want to grab a bunch of flowers and run after a woman in the street, you'll need to have the exact money on you, otherwise you'll have to spend vital seconds entering your PIN number or you'll have to steal the flowers and then have a police officer run romantically after you.

Getting through life safely has a lot in common with crossing the road safely in that before you do anything rash, it's wise to stop, look and listen. You can choose to skip blithely across the dual carriageway of life but don't be surprised when you're hit by the oncoming juggernaut of consequences.

Very occasionally in life you feel like giving a spontaneous whoop of joy. Feel free to whoop but be aware that this is the exact moment when a pillar of the community will emerge from behind a tree. Then, for as long as you live, they will have you marked down as a spontaneous whooper and therefore deeply suspect. If you want to do something expansive, exuberant and spontaneous, wait until you're safely hidden away in the shed, under your duvet or, preferably, both at the same time.

Jazz is spontaneity in musical form. To be good at jazz you have to be a very proficient musician. Similarly, if you want to have a spontaneous, jazz kind of life, you need to be exceptionally well organized underneath. Remember, there's a fine line in life between going with the flow and being flushed down the pan.

How to be Simple

Saying that someone is simple is a little bit insulting, whereas it should be the highest compliment. It's very simple to make things difficult and very difficult to make things simple. Things generally start simple, get difficult and then become simple again. The middle bit is where you learn the value of simplicity and try to regain it.

Human beings are complex and we're drawn to complexity as if to prove just how complex we are. Some people simply wouldn't feel alive unless they were living a horrifically tangled existence. Wealthy people will occasionally hire a life coach to simplify their lives and then end up sleeping with them just to keep things difficult.

Getting simplicity into your life is the same process as good product design: firstly, reduce the number of moving parts; secondly, make the outside user-friendly; and lastly, do one thing really well.

All the great inventions make things more simple, not more complex. There are fortunes to be made in simpler ways to generate power, find love or change a duvet cover.

On the other hand, some things don't work when they're too simple: for example, flamenco, whisky and foreign policy.

Cooking often benefits from simplicity. Top chefs sometimes realize this but then make the mistake of thinking simplicity somehow equates to small portions. It's a simple mistake but an annoying one.

Life is easier when you keep it simple. That's why cults that offer a simpler way of life are so powerful. They promise to put all your complications into one basket and in return let you have one simple and overwhelming debt to them.

Remember that truly simple things don't have small print, they don't have add-ons, they don't have Part Twos, they don't have extended warranties and they don't need anyone to explain them. Technology is rarely simple: when a salesperson claims it is and then takes half an hour to demonstrate, you'll know it isn't. Simple things sell themselves.

Getting one part of your life simple often results in increasing complexity in other parts. Monks who seem to be living simple lives often spend a lot of time producing rich polyphonic music and beautifully complex wines. Never confuse minimalism with simplicity. Minimalism is very clever people pretending to be simple. In reality there's nothing simple about not being able to find somewhere to hang a tea towel.

How to Co-operate

Opinion is divided on whether humans are naturally co-operative or not. The fact that no one seems to be able to agree on this question is a pretty good answer in itself. Because co-operation doesn't come naturally, it requires incredibly complex rules: these take the form of constitutions for societies, marriage vows for relationships and terms and conditions for skip hire.

People are drawn together because some tasks are too big for one person. They say that too many cooks spoil the broth, but they also say that many hands make light work. The trick is to have one person working on the soup and the rest on the electrics.

The best kind of co-operation is when you work with people who are good at what you're bad at and bad at what you're good at. This rarely happens because most jobs require one person being very good at something and the other person holding the ladder.

Mutual self-interest is the real driver of co-operation. Things happen fastest when everyone involved benefits.

The model for this is John Lewis, not Cuba, and the big difference is whether people agree to co-operate or are told to co-operate.

The first step towards mutual co-operation is to listen. For this you have to make the huge act of faith that the other person is not a colossal fathead. Don't forget that the other person is making an equally large allowance for you. Agreeing to disagree is where you understand what the other person thinks but you believe that their ridiculous opinion is based on their fatally flawed character, their weak intellect and their deep-seated selfishness.

An essential part of co-operation therefore is a little give and take. This doesn't mean they give and you take. Rather, it means everyone making a few compromises. A bad compromise is where everyone feels hard done by and a good compromise is where everyone thinks they got away quite lightly.

Some people don't like working with other people because they want to do things their own way. Others see co-operation as a blissful escape from being forced to work on their own. Most small businesses are based on one person doing things his way and the rest of the staff also doing things his way. Your wage packet shows how much you're being paid to co-operate.

20

How to be Modest

It's very difficult to claim that you're brilliant at being modest. People who are genuinely modest constantly struggle with the fact that they are good at being modest. And if someone accuses them of being humble, they'll protest long and loud that they are in fact monstrously arrogant.

The difference between people with store cards and people who are modest is that the latter refuse to take credit for anything. Having single-handedly done something awesome, they will instinctively say it was basically a team effort. When you point out that there wasn't actually a team involved, the modest person then insists anybody could have done what they did. If this fails to staunch the flow of praise, the modest person will insist that they just had a lot of luck or they were just in the right place at the right time.

All this is why trying to praise a seriously modest person can get quite irritating. The praiser on their part is showing considerable humility in being pleased for the modest person instead of being bitter at their success. The least the modest person can do is accept a bit of praise. Too much modesty comes across as quietly smug self-righteousness.

These days there aren't many high-street clothes shops specializing in modest clothing. If you want to dress modestly, then you have to wear work clothing. A woman in a bakery wearing a white coat and hair-net is the closest we get to modesty in appearance. The proof of this is that lingerie shops don't sell bakery worker outfits.

Victorians took modesty a little too far by covering up disgustingly provocative things like piano legs. Now that piano legs are uncovered no one seems to be too excited by them. In fact the more you cover up something, the more exciting it gets. Naturist beaches are probably the least exciting places on earth.

Any culture that worships celebrity is unlikely to value modesty. Modesty will probably go the same way as seemly behaviour, which you can now only find in the Isle of Wight. Marketing people have a problem with the word 'modesty'. Instead, they use words such as authentic, minimalist, artisan or fun-sized. What modesty really needs is a pressure group to promote greater modesty in public life. There probably is one somewhere but they don't want to draw attention to themselves.

How to Cheer People Up

The Grand Old Duke of York was unusual in that he was neither up nor down. Most people often get down and then need a bit of help to cheer up. Doing nice things for people is a way of cheering people up, but be careful: when someone is struggling to hold themselves together, an act of gratuitous niceness can instantly reduce them to tears.

Do not attempt to cheer someone up by telling them that you are suffering more. This will not make them happier, it will just add an icing of irritation on their cake of sadness. Saying that worse things happen at sea is not a good idea either, especially if you're on an expensive cruise at the time.

Telling jokes is a very bad way of cheering people up. If it was a good way, the Samaritans would be famous for their light entertainment. A better way is to recognize that people are not themselves. It shows that you're paying attention, and more often than not it is lack of attention that makes people sad in the first place.

Time is a great healer but with a long waiting list. If you're bent on getting someone cheered up, timing is crucial. Sometimes people need to be brought out of themselves, but only after they've spent some quality time alone within themselves. When someone is emotionally hibernating, don't pull them out into the sunlight, especially if they're a bear.

Naturally jolly people are rubbish at cheering other people up because they can't understand why anybody would be down in the first place. Clowns are great in children's hospitals because kids are naturally cheery, but they are totally counter-productive in adult wards and in fact put their own life in danger as well as the patients.

The medical profession's way of cheering you up is to prescribe anti-depressants. This is like taking Botox internally in that anti-depressants freeze your emotions and limit your capacity to regain your natural smile. Jigsaws are a much better way of cheering yourself up because they totally occupy the mind. Just make sure the completed picture isn't a giant photo of your smirking ex-husband.

Occasionally you can cheer people up by telling them to count their blessings, but think beforehand if they've actually got any, otherwise you'll just be rubbing their nose in it. On the other hand, if they've got to 500 and they're still counting, this can be a bit of a downer for you.

NICE MOVES

How to Wiggle

Pleasure is wiggle-shaped. Think about the last time you wiggled and it's a pretty good bet that you were having fun. Hips that wiggle are attractive because love-making itself is the closest humans get to moving like a caterpillar. If love-making is done on a flat surface and lasts more than two minutes, it's actually an effective form of locomotion (hence the song).

Waggling is a close cousin to wiggling. Some parts of the body are waggled rather than wiggled. For example, you wiggle your toes but waggle your ears. You waggle your wings but wiggle your toggle. You can also toggle your woggle. Interestingly, you can't waggle or wiggle your brain. This has its own special movement – boggling. It's a specialist movement and you won't get far trying to boggle your foot.

Worms are said to be wiggly, but in their natural environment they go straight as a tube train. It's only when you hold them up that they wiggle, but then you'd probably wiggle if someone was holding you

2,000 feet up and you had no hands to cling on with.

Dogs, especially ones in windows, have waggly tails. If you have one with a wiggly tail, check carefully that it isn't in fact a pig. Bees have a waggle dance, which communicates where the honey is to other bees. Human dancing is also a sequence of wiggles and waggles to show other humans where to find the sweet stuff.

Wiggling and waggling should never be done continuously as they lose their signalling potency. Continuous waggling becomes waddling, a far less attractive proposition. Similarly, there is a danger that wiggling done too fast becomes jiggling and no one likes that. 'Get a wiggle on' now means to hurry up. This should not be confused with 'get a woggle on', which means joining a scouting movement.

No situation in life is so desperate that there isn't room left to wiggle. Some people, who do very little else in life, show extraordinary energy and ingenuity when it comes to wiggling out of things.

Top physicists say that the smallest particles of the universe are super-strings that wiggle. It's great to know that even when you're absolutely motionless waiting for a bus, the whole universe is wiggling away. Even DNA, the stuff of life, is just two wiggling wiggles.

How to Skip

Skipping is what you do when you want to jump for joy but need to get from A to B at the same time. Skipping is how knees laugh. Like sidestroke in the swimming pool, you can actually move pretty quickly skipping but you look a bit of an idiot doing it.

The opposite feeling to skipping is sinking. Interestingly, your heart skips a beat just before you get a sinking feeling. Getting stones to skip over water is intensely satisfying because for a moment they skip rather than sink. It must be the ultimate thrill for stones.

Boxers incorporate skipping into their training routine; it works out the trapezius muscles and also, when someone calls you a big girl's blouse for skipping, you get a practice fight laid on for you.

Skipping is happiness in motion. That's why you don't see a lot of it at funerals unless someone knows that the will is looking exceptionally good for them. It's also why the father generally accompanies the bride down the aisle so she doesn't skip all the way and trip over her train in an inappropriate and undignified manner.

Animals don't skip. That's because skipping doesn't fulfil any of the functions important to animals: feeding, fighting, fleeing or firkling. When humans skip, it's highly unlikely they're doing any of the above either.

The triple jump is basically a hop, a skip and a jump, but they changed the name because skipping didn't sound much like an Olympic sport (that's pretty rich when they've got beach volleyball). Falling in love is like the triple jump: the even pace of life is suddenly disrupted by a sudden upward movement; you then skip with happiness; before leaping into the relationship sandpit.

When you look at your life, it's instructive to see what internal gait you favour: are you a trudger, leaper, dancer, dragger, loper, sprinter or plodder? Skippers are the most blessed in life. It's what God would do if he wasn't obliged to be everywhere at once.

People love skipping. If it said skip the rest of this, you probably would. Skipping over things is one of life's great pleasures. There is no rule that says you have to start at the beginning and work your way through to the end. And if there was a rule that said that, you could skip it.

How to Turn

People who know exactly where they're going are rare in life and generally rather frightening. Life happens in a series of diversions from where you thought you were going. Turning is perfectly natural and the worst thing that can happen is that you have nowhere left to turn. In fact, that's a very good definition of a dead end.

British roads are designed on the principle that one good turn deserves another. Cities are normally based on grids leaving all the turning work up to you. What black-cab drivers like more than anything else is doing U-turns. A black cab has the turning circle of a vole and most cabbies will tell you that five years doing THE KNOWLEDGE is worth it just to be able to U-turn in a space that would require a fifty-eight-point turn in a normal car.

All fairground rides work because we find turning exciting and slightly scary at the same time. In fact all dances are based on the same principle. The only exception is modern dancing, which has banished twirling, turning and spinning. Secretly everyone still wants to turn but doesn't want to be seen as some kind of disco/jive relic.

Most people turn when they get to a corner. More interesting are the people who turn when there is no corner. These are the people who invent the new corners. Many get lost doing it but that's the way the guiding grids of life are formed. One of the reasons Americans are so direct is their historical notion of the frontier. This gives rise to the deep-set belief that you don't have to turn to get anywhere, you just have to push on a little further.

You can turn right or turn left. However, if you turn one way three times, it's actually the same as turning the other way. Remember this if you are driving in a big city for the first time or intend to have a lengthy political career.

You can turn things on and off and up and down. You can also turn them over when you're looking for the on switch. People can also be turned on. If instead someone turns you off, you can turn them down. Or if you're in bed, you can turn over. When you use sophisticated computer-modelling to overlay all possible turns, the three-dimensional shape created looks amazingly like a turnip. Which is a bit of a turn-up.

How to Spin

Human entertainment often seems to take the form of spinning – maypoles, carousels and most dances involve spinning. That's because spinning puts us back in touch with our inner electron. Spinning is exciting because it's a way of getting the maximum possible movement in the smallest possible space. If dances didn't involve spinning, dance halls would have to be a lot bigger.

Everything in the universe is spinning, from vast galaxies to subatomic particles. The sun spins too, but because it isn't solid, different parts spin at different speeds much like an accomplished belly dancer. Dizziness is the feeling that things are spinning too fast. It can be assuaged by focusing on something moving at the same speed. On a carousel this would be the horse in front; in a Viennese Waltz it would be your partner's ear.

Spinning seems to be vital to our civilization. Clothing comes from spinning, fire can be spun and most power is generated by something spinning, from windmills to electromagnets. We then use the power to make other things spin, from bus wheels to garden strimmers. At a cosmic level the great wheel of life is always spinning gently, slow enough for us not to notice but just too fast to get off.

When something spins really fast, it appears to be very still. This is an illusion as you will soon discover if you try to empty a spin-dryer mid-cycle. The Whirling Dervishes of Turkey use spinning as a way of ritual purification. Candy floss is manufactured in the same way except that the bad spin-offs are put on a stick and eaten.

There aren't many organic things that spin because the engineering's quite complex. Just think how useful it would be if your hand spun and how many expensive kitchen utensils you could dispense with. Spiders spin webs at incredible speed, which is one of the reasons they have to sit very still in their web afterwards to get over the sick feeling.

Politicians have developed a particular taste for spinning. If they don't think something will appeal to the electorate, they will spin it until a more acceptable face is presented. What they forget is that when you start something spinning, it continues to spin until you can see its bare behind.

How to be High

Mountains are a natural high. You can look down at the valleys beneath and see how insignificant we really are (don't go too high or you get to the death zone, which is where nature proves how insignificant we are by killing us). Spending time in the moral high ground has a similar bracing effect for the self-righteous.

In life you get the height of fashion and sophistication, although you also get the height of stupidity which – hardly surprising – resides on the same mountain top. Far below you have the depths of depravity, despair and Gloucestershire. The main attraction of 4×4s is not driving up mountains but sitting high enough to look over garden fences. If there were a 12×4 car that carried four people twelve foot high so you could see in people's bedrooms, this would be even more popular.

Feeling up or down is largely due to our relationship with the great and ancient god of gravity. Once space travel becomes the norm, it will be inadvisable for the depressed to travel to large planets because their hearts will feel even heavier.

A breath of fresh air always makes you feel slightly better because it increases your natural buoyancy. Sighing, on the other hand, is nature's way of discharging your ballast tanks like a submarine to make you sink lower. We all carry the world on our shoulders; it's called our head and it too is round, continually turning and teeming with life. When you've got the world on your shoulders, just be glad it's not on your foot.

Drug-taking is a way of getting as high as a kite. Kite-flying itself is equally effective with similar ups and downs but markedly less long-term paranoia. Some prescription drugs cancel out life's highs and lows by smoothing everything out. These drugs have been very successful, and it makes you wonder if the person who invented them is very happy about it or doesn't really feel anything.

There are some people who seem to be naturally high on life without any form of artificial stimulant. They don't even seem to be crying inside. However, nature has to balance things up and you'll generally find the corresponding misery in the people who have to spend a lot of time with them.

How to Sparkle

The spark is the prime mover, the thing that gets things started. Universes, prairie fires, unstoppable revolutions and passionate loves are ignited by sparks, but no one is quite sure how the cosmic spark plug works. The sparkiest scientific minds in the most sparkling laboratories are dedicated to finding the source of the spark.

More importantly, the sparkly boob tube allows the average woman to feel like a jewel-bedecked queen of the orient without having to have an oppressive and hierarchical social structure in place to facilitate the mining, cutting and polishing of rare gems. Women also look for a sparkle in their men, not in their jewellery but in their eyes. A sparkly-eyed man can laugh any woman into bed (a woman can also laugh any man out of bed but that's a different story).

Humans, like magpies, are attracted to things that sparkle, from rubies on their fingers to metallic paint on their Audis. In a restaurant you always feel you should choose sparkling water because it sounds so much more exciting and glamorous, even though you know it will make you belch like a volcano. Champagne's sparkle somehow suggests you're more successful just by drinking it.

Our love of sparkling is intimately bound up with sun worship. Sparkling snow and sparkling sea look so good because they are being kissed by the sun. Fake tan is an attempt by humans to look similarly sun-kissed, but the actual impression often tends to be more mud-slathered.

The opposite of sparkling is matt black. Goths tend to fight shy of wearing any kind of sequin, although, if they're not careful, the sun can sparkle merrily off their line of ear piercings. The tragic decline of Elvis was marked by the migration of the sparkle from his eyes to the rhinestones on his jumpsuit. Far worse than having no sparkle is losing your sparkle. Old cola, Morecambe, black holes and the Greek royal family: they've all lost their sparkle, and nothing's flatter than that.

Sparks have their dark sides. Most sparks never become a flame. They do nothing but illuminate the depth of the darkness for a second and are gone. On the other hand a really big spark, like a bolt of lightning or a night of searing passion, will make you forget the darkness for a very long time to come.

How to be Soft

L ife is hard, which is why soft things are so popular. Most people, even really hard ones, love soft furnishings. The only people who don't are religious cults who believe squishiness is the work of the devil. Shakers are famous for their hard chairs. They're called Shakers because they can never get comfortable.

In general, women are soft on the outside and tough on the inside. Men are tough on the outside and soft on the inside. Marriage balances this all out. Women are then soft on the inside and men are in the shed.

Most people have a soft spot for someone. When they're around, you feel slightly gooey inside like an undercooked sponge. You should never tell someone you have a soft spot for them. Soft spots are by their nature too soft to do anything with.

The Bible very wisely speaks of the 'soft word that turns away wrath'. Unfortunately they don't tell you what that useful soft word is, but it could well be 'tea?'. Softness is stronger than hardness. In order to be your most effective you have to relax – and that means letting your mind and body go soft. That's when you become really powerful. Be aware that this doesn't apply to motorcycle display teams.

War is when men hit each other with hard things. Softness always wins in the end, but that's not much consolation when you're being hit by a very hard thing. Generally, they say that it's a good thing to speak softly and carry a big stick. Make sure the stick is a hard one and not a big soft one, otherwise you'll look a bit of a chump.

Being hard-headed is good but too much of it and you become bone-headed. Similarly, a soft heart is good but being a soft touch isn't. Softness by itself doesn't work. No one, for example, wants to sleep on a bean bag; rubber tyres are useless without steel rims; sofas need wooden frames; flesh needs a skeleton; fondant centres need chocolate shells; reproduction is tricky with totally soft genitals.

Man is the tool-bearing animal, which means we know how to use hard things in a soft world. Cutting, hitting, digging and stacking got us out of the caves. But what advanced mankind seems to want in the end is slippers, woolly jumpers and soft furnishings, which, strangely, most animals have built-in.

How to Burn

Kindling fire was one of the turning points of human evolution right up there with learning how to put it out. Fire was vitally important to early man as it gave warmth for heating and cooking, light for protection and homework, and charcoal for cave paintings and barbecues.

According to the Ancient Greeks, Prometheus was the man who first stole fire from the gods. Mankind was then punished for this theft by being sent woman for the first time in the shape of Pandora. This says something very significant about either fire or women or the Ancient Greeks.

One of the secret attractions of cigarettes is the fact that you burn them. They wouldn't be half so attractive if you had to take nicotine via a suppository. The fact that you have to light up is in itself comforting as you are in effect standing round your own one-person campfire. Pipes had an even more comforting effect because it was like building your own bonfire and setting light to it.

Fire-fighters have an almost mythic status in our society because they tackle the uncontrolled forces of nature. It's the same with lifeboat crew. If traffic wardens also dealt with tornadoes and bad flooding, they might enhance their status somewhat.

Fire often gets a bad press possibly because it can destroy cities in one big night out. On the other hand there's nothing nicer than sitting round a roaring log fire on a cold winter's night. The trick is to make sure the latter doesn't become the former. Fire is like a naughty child: quite cute to begin with but liable to get out of hand if not kept well under control.

It is possible to burn without a flame. For example, you can burn with desire. You can also burn with a fever. These two are remarkably similar in that they both make you feel very hot and slightly delirious. The cure for both is bed and complete rest/passion.

Watching flames dance is an elemental and deeply moving experience and it's no wonder many native tribes like the Comanche and the 2nd Faringdon Brownies like to perform sacred rituals around them. Fire can have a purging cathartic effect, except for a firing squad, which is more permanent and less life-enhancing.

How to Melt

Melting into someone's arms is to understand for a moment the internal life of chocolate. Feelings of spiritual and physical ecstasy are remarkably like melting into the universe until you are at one with it. Scientifically, you become a sort of cosmic emulsion.

Everyone has a boiling point where they get angry but also a melting point where, if you apply enough kindness, they suddenly go soppy and become completely malleable. The melting of a hardened heart is a wonderful thing. It proves that love is not a solid.

Melting is closely associated with sensual pleasure, although the opposite of melting, solidification, also has sexual connotations. It may be that sensual pleasure simply comes from moving from one state to another. This would help explain why so many find musicals on ice, fondues and candles strangely compelling (though not all at once).

Chocolate, apart from tasting yummy, has the remarkable property of melting at body temperature. It will happily melt in your mouth, which is one of the reasons we're so keen to put it there. It would be interesting to know if cabbage would be more popular if it too melted in the mouth.

We humans tend to worry about melting. Molten lava really scares us as it reminds us that the solid old earth is just bubbling liquid underneath, although we're quite pleased when all this lava cools, leaving a palm-fringed atoll. Sadly most of these atolls will soon be submerged by the ice caps melting.

Melting is a pleasure more appreciated in this country than others. That's because our weather teeters between freeze and thaw, rather than having one of each per year. Our national emotional temperature is the same, finely balanced between cool indifference and warm sentimentality with a million mini-melts in between.

Nuclear power is supposed to be generated in a solid state and melting is therefore unwelcome. Meltdown is worse than breakdown because it implies that the thing can never be reconstituted in its original shape. A bar of chocolate can be broken down, but leaving it in the sun will lead to an irretrievable meltdown. Death is the ultimate meltdown although no one's quite sure what state it leads to. Ideally we would all end up as chocolate and then be consumed by worthy people in another life.

How to be Vague

Vague is out of vogue in our high-definition age. However, there is an unwritten rule (until now) that the more clearly defined something is, the less satisfying it becomes. The higher-definition your TV becomes, the less you watch it. Naturally this First Rule of Vagueness only applies to some things in some places at some times.

Vagueness by definition can't be defined. As long as people have a vague notion of what it means, that's enough. Science likes to define everything, but increasingly the big brains are finding that the interesting stuff happens in the vague areas between what's already been defined.

The same theory works in life generally: you have a few big concrete facts and the rest is just a vague kind of splodginess in between. This can be a slough of despond or a blancmange of happiness depending on how lucky you are. Memories are often vague but in reality are quite accurate because things often happen rather vaguely in the first place. It's the crystal-clear memories that tend to mislead you.

Some people exist in a kind of watercolour life where everything seems to blur and bleed into everything else. Their timekeeping is usually poor, their food tends towards the risotto and they wear clothes in a strangely undefined way. From their ranks, great business leaders seldom spring.

Only extremists reject vagueness and insist on seeing things in black and white. They generally have a very stark idea of what they want in this life or the next. For everyone else, life is more of a thick grey fog through which our heads occasionally pop, revealing a flash of clear blue sky.

Language originally developed in order to combat vagueness and aid precise communication. It's difficult to work together and build an advanced civilization when nobody really knows what anybody else is talking about. In recent years this process has been reversed. Modern speech shies away from the defined and instead is based on three squishy pillars of vagueness: 'you know', 'kind of' and 'whatever' – not helpful for large civil-engineering projects.

Vagueness can actually be a useful tool because it forces other people to define things for you. When you meet people, try asking them, 'How's your thing going?' You'll be amazed at the variety, richness and intimacy of the responses.

LOVING FEELINGS

How to Find Love

Finding love is the opposite to crossing the road – you only make progress when you stop looking. The reason for this is that people always look for love in the wrong place. It's like crossing the road on the continent – you get run over by love when you're looking the wrong way.

Many people have an ideal of what they're looking for in a partner. Often this ideal gets in the way of finding a real partner. If you're searching for a tall dark stranger, you might well be looking precisely six inches above the short pale friend who is your real soul-mate.

An ever-growing number of people find love online. The internet is a masked ball for the socially challenged. The advantage of love online is that you can choose from many more people. The drawback is you then have to fly to Cuba to meet them. Also remember that you're highly unlikely to meet rugged outdoors types on the net.

When you're looking for love, you view the whole world as emotional hypertext and everyone in it as someone you can possibly click with to find a deeper level of meaning. Remember when you've finally found someone to turn your search engine off.

Being set up by your friends is always alarming, not because you might meet the Swamp Thing on your date but because of the realization that your friends think your ideal partner is the Swamp Thing. For their part, the Swamp Thing feels the same about you, and this feeling of shared anger can often lead to a successful relationship with them and the end of your relationship with your so-called friends.

Love only comes to you when you give out the big confident love vibe. That's why it's very difficult to find love when you're depressed and miserable. This fact alone is often enough to make you more depressed and miserable. You then get desperate and go out with someone totally unsuitable, which makes you utterly miserable. At this stage you take a vow of chastity, which bizarrely is generally the first step to a fulfilling love life.

When you finally find love, it generally comes in two forms: the first makes you cry a lot but feel incredibly alive; the second makes you laugh a lot and feel incredibly relaxed. Either form is fine as long as you're both having the same experience.

How to Broach Things

Everyone has one or two subjects in their life that sooner or later will need broaching. Generally one of the subjects you'll need to broach with someone else and the other subject someone will need to broach with you. Occasionally these broachings coincide in either the most pleasurable or the most painful day of your life.

Men only broach things five or six times in their entire life: can I have a pocket-money/salary raise; will you go out with me; will you marry me; are you seeing another man; I think you've tucked your skirt into your pants. Any one of these broachings can change a man's life irretrievably. That's why men don't normally volunteer to talk about new things unless it really is the final option.

Women broach matters in an entirely different way. Generally the first a man hears about a vital topic is when the woman says something like: 'You know that thing we agreed last week?' Women swim in a vast ocean of seamless communication on all levels with possibilities washing in and out with the tide. On their side, men often feel like the little Dutch boy with his finger in the dyke. If they pull their finger out and broach a new subject, then the ocean will be let in and it will seem like a hell of a long time before it goes out again.

Timing your broach is half the battle. That means the target is not hungry and irritable, but neither are they very sleepy because they've had too much pudding or hyper-active because they've had too much sugar. The target should not have just arrived/be about to leave, be in the shower, getting dressed or putting up a shelf because this then gives them the opportunity to say 'Look, I've just got in, I'm putting up a shelf, etc.'

Often what you want to broach is so scary you need to camouflage it with a protective cordon of bushes around which you can then beat. Sometimes beating around the bush is useful because it gives the target a signal that something important is about to happen. However, bush-beating becomes seriously irritating to the target after approximately five minutes regardless of sugar levels.

Once you've broached something, it's impossible to unbroach it. It's very difficult to pretend you didn't ask someone to marry you or that you didn't want to try naturism on your next holiday. Instead, the only low-risk way of broaching things is to lay out a smorgasbord of hypothetical scenarios. Try to make all the other options equally credible, otherwise it's going to be pretty clear that you heavily favour the naturist mini-break.

How to Write a Love Letter

A love letter is a normal letter with everything taken out except the 'Dear' at the beginning and the 'With love' at the end. The rest of the letter then elaborates on these two bits.

Love letters are traditionally drenched in perfume. You should use a sufficient quantity that archaeologists in a thousand years' time are still in no doubt about your feelings. The male equivalent of perfume is blood, particularly your own or that of a close rival.

The golden rule with love letters is not to write about yourself. It shouldn't read like a job application or a newsletter. The only exception is to write about how you feel about them. Ideally there should be a 'you' every seven words.

There are three main subjects for the bulk of a love letter: how wonderful they are, how much you love them and how long your love will last. A love letter fails unless the answers to these three are 'very', 'a lot' and 'forever'. Missing one is a big mistake. For example, 'I love you like the perfect storm and will continue to do so until next week.' This won't cut the romantic mustard.

When you start a letter, you should never use someone's name. 'To the pincushion of my heart' is going to carry more weight than 'Dear Simon'. It also alerts them that the letter is not going to be demanding repayment of tax credits or some such.

Proper love letters are read on average five times an hour. The best lines will be read twice as often. The reader will also be searching for hidden meaning. You don't actually have to hide any meaning when you write because they will find plenty anyway.

Always remember that your love letters will be read by a wide circle of close friends and acquaintances as putting 'Private and Confidential' on a handwritten letter is the equivalent of clicking 'Forward to All' on an email.

It's best to write love letters by hand. This shows you care enough to find a pen. However, most love letters these days are sent by email or text. The advantage of this is you don't have to wait for the postman and you can send them to multiple recipients. The disadvantage is that you're never going to soar on the wings of poetic ecstasy with Ur Gr8.

How to Bond

Women are very good at bonding. The way they do this is by swapping the innermost secrets of their relationships with their mothers, their partners and their fridge. Women also bond by commenting on each other's clothing and accessories, especially if an item is on display for the first time. Comments have to fall within the very positive to ecstatic range. 'You've made a bad mistake with those earrings' doesn't aid female bonding and is a comment best left for men to deliver towards the very end of their relationship.

Advanced female bonding can involve the borrowing of clothing and accessories, but this has to be done with discretion. If your friend is wearing a new top she's very pleased with, she won't want to lend it to you that evening for the party you're both going to. Suggesting it could lead to unbonding.

Male bonding is a very delicate manoeuvre done in a very masculine way. It requires overcoming the instinctive competition between males and replacing it with a state of loving co-operation without ever implying that there's any hint of homosexuality between the men involved. Oddly enough, the quickest way to bond for some men is to fight. This proves that both are strong masculine figures and allows them to get to grips with each other in a totally heterosexual manner. It's important when fighting not to knock your partner out cold as this gets the relationship off to a somewhat shaky start.

Men mostly bond by doing things that involve standing and looking in the same direction together. That's why watching football and drinking at a bar are two of the favourites. Standing at a bar watching football on TV is the quickest possible way of bonding. Golf is how older men bond by walking in the same direction together. If golf involved one person starting from each end of the course and racing to get round, it wouldn't be nearly as effective.

Sex is a great way of bonding between men and women as it releases a powerful hormone which encourages chocolate purchase. Bonding between men and women without sex is quite tricky unless the woman can stand next to the man and then talk about the intimate details of an affair she's currently having with a leading football player.

How to Have a Row

Some people don't feel real communication is happening unless it's at maximum volume. Having a good row shows that you've got some important things to get over and can actually be a lot healthier than icy indifference. Although when you live with a habitual shouter, you'd sometimes give your right arm for a bit of icy indifference.

To row properly, 90 per cent of sentences need to start with the word 'You' followed by a grievous sin on their part. Using 'I' is a sure sign that you're losing the argument and are about to apologize, unless the 'I' is swiftly followed by 'don't give a monkey's'.

Throwing things adds a three-dimensional element to rowing. If you find yourself throwing things underarm and your opposite number is catching them easily, then you're probably not putting your heart into it. Never argue with a professional knife-thrower in a kitchen. Wait until you're both in a soft-play area.

Rows are mini emotional typhoons; they arrive

suddenly and depart equally suddenly but do an enormous amount of damage in between. Another word for 'typhoons' is 'twisters' because everything that is said is totally twisted to gain maximum possible destructive power.

You shouldn't attempt to have a row if you don't have previous experience, otherwise you'll just end up hurting yourself. Similarly, trying to have a row with someone who doesn't row is like trying to play tennis with somebody standing on the same side of the net as you are. It's not much of a sport.

Done well, rowing is exactly the same as relationship counselling except on fast-forward with added expletives. The result is much the same in that everything is aired, examined and pulled to pieces and everyone goes away feeling much better. When habitual rowers decide to have a mature and calm conversation, this generally signals the end of the relationship.

In general, the British aren't as good at arguing as other nations. To begin with, we're all rather shy when it comes to expressing ourselves. Secondly, expressing ourselves tends towards violence without much build-up. And thirdly, we know we're right so there's not much to argue about.

Rows finish in one of two ways: great sex or epic sulking. Never attempt to have great sex with someone who is epically sulking. This will immediately provoke another row in which accusations of sexual harassment will feature largely.

How to be Happy

Happiness is like a scooter; once you're up and running, you can just scoot along. It's getting up in the first place that's the tricky bit. Happiness needs to be kick-started and the secret of doing this is to stop your brain working. Given its head, as it were, the brain likes to prove how intelligent it is by being miserable. Have you noticed how intellectuals tend to be glum because it looks so much cleverer than walking around whistling like the village idiot?

Happiness is all about forgetting yourself and realizing that it's a beautiful world out there. (Don't confuse this with forgetting things, because if you rush out into the beautiful world and forget your keys, you're not going to be happy for long.) Meeting together with a party of like-minded women to sort out three tons of copper collected for charity will get your hands very dirty, but halfway through, when everyone's working away and the jokes about spending a penny are flowing thick and fast, a lovely feeling will set in. That's happiness.

Music is the food of happiness: if you catch yourself whistling, humming or singing to yourself, you are happy. The best workout for making yourself happy is to sing songs in the bath at high volume because filling your lungs full of air is a short cut to happiness. Miserable people don't like breathing; they smoke, slump around and mumble. If they were to stand up straight, take big breaths, speak clearly and exercise regularly, they would be very happy. They wouldn't have any friends but, boy, would they be happy.

One of the drawbacks of being happy and knowing it is that you feel an urge to clap your hands. Never reply 'I'm very happy' when someone asks you how you are, as it gives the impression that you are one step away from madness, religious conversion or both. Virtually all behaviour associated with happiness such as whooping, skipping, hugging and whistling is frowned upon in public unless it's been induced by alcohol or by being five years old. That's why train passengers generally look as though they're all off to the annual conference of the terminally miserable.

The only way you can be sure someone is happy is that they make you feel happy too. Unhappy people make other people unhappy often to prove just how unhappy they really are. Happiness is quietly infectious – it's the virus that dare not speak its name.

How to be Good in Bed

Making love to somebody who thinks they're good in bed is like doing a yoga class on fast-forward. Just when you're getting into the swing of one position, you're being wrestled into a new one. Changing position once you've started sex is actually dangerous and unnecessary. You wouldn't change driving position once a car was moving, so why on earth would you do it in bed.

Everyone has their favourite position for love-making. For most men it is woman on top. For most women, it is woman on her side under duvet with man in airing cupboard hanging out laundry. There is a position after a furious bout of love-making where you lie totally still, side by side in a kind of satisfied silence. This position is what married people do instead of a furious bout of love-making.

People who think they're good in bed often insist on dragging accessories into bed with them. You can be quietly enjoying yourself and suddenly you're expected to get busy with a food-blender, strimmer or wallpaper table.

If you're a woman and you don't want to accessorize, simply whisper 'later' into your lover's ear. Nine times out of ten there won't be a later.

For a man to be good in bed the golden rule is not to get into bed. Instead, you have to spend a lot of time in restaurants and shops. This all counts as foreplay. Once you finally get down to it, the trick is not to get down to it and instead concentrate on kissing. Women like kissing and they're generally not happy unless they're coated head to foot in slobber.

Interestingly, for women to be good in bed, they only have to kiss a man lightly on the cheek. When the man tells his mates in the pub about it the next day, the woman will have become an absolute minx. It's very difficult for a woman to be good in bed when the man is rubbish. It's like being good at football but no one passing you the ball (as it were).

Talking about what you're going to do to each other when you get to bed can often be a very good form of foreplay. Run what you're going to say through your mind before you say it, and if you can only come up with one three-word sentence, saying it might actually be counter-productive.

Everyone knows about foreplay but afterplay is equally important. This is where you kiss your partner, tell her how much you love her and then wrench her entire duvet off.

How to End a Relationship

Chucking someone is a form of murder. Instead of wanting them to cease to exist in their life, you want them to cease to exist in your life. When chucking people, you have to decide whether you're going to be nice or nasty. Remember that being nice often turns out to be nastier in the long run.

A nice way of chucking someone is to say, 'It's nothing to do with you, it's me that's the problem.' This is actually quite a tricky approach because you're the one they like. You then have to pretend to have become someone quite different with different needs. But this makes you even more interesting as you suddenly become 'old partner with exciting new dimensions'. The next step is then to clarify in what precise way you have changed into this new person. This breaks down into needing more time, more space or more sex with other people. You generally have to work your way through the first two excuses before you admit to the third.

The nasty route involves telling your partner in detail

how much you hate them. Although this process reflects badly on your taste in partners to begin with, the purgative effect of denouncing them is well worth the price. However, this approach also has its risks. For a start, you can feel so good after telling them what a bastard they are that you end up having the best sex of your life. Also, if you really tell your partner what a clinging tiresome drag they are, they can immediately demonstrate the truth of this by clinging on to your leg when you try to leave.

A great way of chucking people is to do it the same way business does it. Call them in and tell them that you're going to have to let them go. Explain that their individual competencies don't match your overall strategic direction. Or you can set an arbitrary deadline for them to meet agreed targets for emotional delivery. Then you can point out that they've missed their targets, their deadline and their opportunity to build a long-term future with you.

Always chuck someone at their place or somewhere neutral. It's very difficult to chuck someone at your house and then have to give them a lift to the station, as this will restart the cycle of pleasantness. The best kind of chucking happens in airport departure lounges where you can use lines like, 'Of course I'll wait for you, Tony.' After you've said this, you must wait at least until Tony has got through passport control before you rush off to meet Adam in the short-stay car park.

How to be Broken-Hearted

The downside of giving someone your heart, as with any precious object, is that they may return it broken. It takes two years to become functional again after a broken heart and seven years to really get over someone (substitute days for years if you are fifteen or under).

The answer to the question 'what becomes of the broken-hearted?' is that they mope. Moping is how you move physically when your heart is eight times heavier than normal. Sometimes, when the weather's nice, people go into the garden to mope. These are called lawn mopers.

When a heart breaks, it's the lungs that normally get a good work-out. Sobbing is emotional coughing and it's a great way of getting someone out of the system. Sobbing can be uncontrollable and you just have to let the storm pass. But sometimes you can hear yourself sobbing and a small voice says to you, 'That is a very silly noise.' If you hear that voice, you know you're going to be all right.

Often the hardest loves to forget are the ones that were the most unpleasant. A love so big that it nearly destroyed you is likely to remain with you longer than a love so small it only kept you together once a week for tea. When you break up, you can either heap abuse on the other person or you can say there were irregularities in the interpersonal dynamics. Remember it's much easier to forget irregularities in interpersonal dynamics.

Love affairs are the saturated fat of emotional life and can cause heart problems throughout life. A quadruple heart bypass of friends, alcohol, exercise and food generally work wonders. Rebound relationships often start when you're in emotional free fall. As many wise old parachutists will tell you, it's best to wait until you get your feet on the ground before you decide on your next jump.

Having a broken heart is like being a fan of a very bad football club. You suffer continual heartache but you can't start being a fan of someone else, as that would seem intensely disloyal. The solution in both cases is to take up badminton.

Helpful people will also give you advice such as take it one day at a time. This is very good advice, otherwise you might be tempted to take it five days at a time. When you've just broken up, it's best to make a clean break of it. Don't write or call or text or email or communicate in any way. Maybe just a quick call to tell them you won't be communicating, but that's it.

How to Settle Down

Settling down is what happens when you find yourself in the quicksand of life: at first you can't quite believe you're in it; then you thrash around desperately for a bit; and finally you decide it's not worth struggling and very soon you disappear without trace.

Getting a mortgage is financial quicksand in that it looks like a solid enough thing to do but then sucks you down for the next sixty years. It's called getting on the property ladder to give the impression that you're going higher and higher. A better mental image would be a ladder leading down into a bottomless pit marked 'debt' with estate agents greasing the rungs.

One of the signs of settling down is you consider getting a pension. If you haven't already been paying into a plan since you were twelve, then it's probably too late and you should get used to the fact that you're going to be spending your retirement digging for edible roots.

Settling down often refers to marriage and children. Getting married is second only to divorce in terms of trauma and having children is like having a neutron bomb going off in your life. Why that's called 'settling down' is an absolute mystery. Being beautifully single, spending quality time watching TV in your onesie – now that's a much better definition of settling down properly.

One thing that can be quite depressing is when you feel like it's time to settle down but you haven't yet done anything even remotely unsettled; you don't even know what wild oats are, let alone how you sow them. Happily, there are evening classes to help people sow their wild oats. They're not actually called Intermediate Wild Oat Sowing but taking any evening class will have the desired effect.

People who have upset tummies often take something to settle their stomach. This is normally something dull like bread or chalky tablets. In the same way you can settle your personality by taking up something dull like gardening or rambling. In the same way you wouldn't take drugs before you have an illness, don't take up rambling before you need to settle. Otherwise you will actually find the whole process (and people) deeply unsettling.

If you feel a strong urge to settle down and you don't have a partner, let alone children, a small furry animal can do a lot of the work for you or, more precisely, you can do a lot of the work for it. As one of the key parts of settling down is finding a cast-iron excuse not to socialize, a Scottie dog will work as well as a Snottie tot.

OUT AND ABOUT

How to Have a Nice Day

It's impossible for the British to say 'have a nice day' without the long shadow of sarcasm passing over the conversation. In this country we presume that the day will be bad if not disastrous, whereas in America nice days and the having thereof are written into the constitution.

You only get really good days about once a year. That's when everything in life conspires to be in your favour. Some people worry so much that it will come to an end that they don't enjoy the day when it's there. Just accept that sometimes it really is your day.

Nice days are ones that make happy memories. One nice day can extinguish the memory of thirteen bad ones, which is handy because this is normally the ratio you get on two weeks' holiday with the family. It's also the day you forget your camera.

Nice days can happen spontaneously. You get out of bed on the right side, with a spring in your step and a song in your heart. This can be disconcerting for naturally grumpy people and they have to commit several acts of unpleasantness before the pleasant feeling subsides.

Bad news comes in threes but so does good news. Nice days that start well are likely to get even better and probably end on a high note. You know you've had a good day when you go to bed with a smile on your face. Really good days end with two people smiling in your bed, one of which is you.

There is normally a meteorological aspect to nice days. A shaft of sunlight can for a moment lend a cathedral-like grandeur to a corner of your living room. Sometimes a warm breeze in your hair or the smell of wood smoke can lift your spirits. If you get both at the same time, be careful that your hair is not actually on fire, as this would then begin to be a bad day.

There would be more nice days if everyone made more of an effort to make other people's day. The equivalent of a shaft of sunlight in your living room is sharing a smile or a laugh with a complete stranger. So it's worth smiling at people you meet and, don't worry, with those teeth no one's going to mistake you for an American.

How to Give Directions

It's worrying to think that at any given time 25 per cent of road users aren't really sure where they're going, but what's really chilling is that when you stop for directions, 90 per cent of people you ask haven't a clue either but nevertheless give full instructions of how to get there.

Foreigners get lost easily and often ask for directions. They pull up and ask 'Where is Mayotts Rd?', whereupon two things happen: you realize that you've never heard of Mayotts Rd and they realize that they don't speak English. In an ideal world you would say 'I don't know', they would say 'I don't understand', and then they would drive off and everyone would be happy.

Instead, you give directions to anywhere you can think of that a foreigner would be likely to be going at that time of day and they nod in a painful way and wonder what this 'roundabout' is you mention so often. Finally, with much embarrassment all round, they roar off up a cul-de-sac and then drive back past you three minutes later slumped so low in their seats it looks as if no one is driving.

An amazing thing happens when you ask for directions. You immediately start nodding and stop listening. When you drive off, you both say 'What did he say?' and you realize that neither of you heard a word the man said but you both noticed his luxuriant nasal hair. Even if you do listen, it's impossible to take in any road directions with more than three elements. People can only absorb left, right, straight over – after that your mental road map goes blank.

Remember when you ask directions that you're speaking to a pedestrian who is thinking like a pedestrian. When they say 'Second right, third left', you'll be counting tarmacked sign-posted roads, they'll be counting bridle-ways and holes in hedges, which is why where you want to go is fifty yards away and where you end up is fifty miles away.

If you're asking for directions, never pick on people who look starved of social interaction. As they never go anywhere, they won't know how to get anywhere, but that won't stop them having an hour-long conversation with you, getting your atlas out, settling down in your back seat and helping themselves to your flask of coffee.

How to be Cautious

Caution is shrink-wrapped fear. The quickest way to kill yourself on an escalator is to be too cautious. It's the same in life generally, although with life you don't have to carry dogs and stand to the right.

Caution is what happens when you follow your liver instead of your heart. It's a non-stick emotional surface for the bad things that life throws at you. Sadly, if you're too cautious, the good things that life throws won't stick either.

Cautious people never put their eggs in one basket. Really cautious people make sure they have more than one basket, and also refuse to count their chickens, let alone their eggs. The net result of all this caution, ironically, is that you end up living life on eggshells.

There are two types of cautions: one warns of danger such as 'Caution, Vehicle Reversing!'; the other you get from the police when you reverse over someone. Bad drivers should have a little alert that shouts 'Caution, Idiot Driving!' every time they start up.

Caution in love is fatal. It has the same effect as deploying your parachute before you've left the aircraft. With love-making the opposite is true: it's an excellent idea to deploy all sorts of precautions before you move a muscle.

Precautions are sensible steps you take when you're feeling cautious. Postcautions are sensible steps you take after you've failed to be cautious. Postcautions are generally not as useful as precautions but do benefit from a more precise knowledge of what the danger was.

Cautious optimists are really pessimists who are having a good day. They're clearly worried that something awful is still going to happen. Don't even pretend to be optimistic if you can't be boundless with it.

Children used to be educated through cautionary tales illustrating the catastrophic effects of walking through woods, sucking your thumb, etc. Today we have advertising instead, which tells you how using anything from car insurance to bathroom cleaner can lead to unimaginable happiness. It's not much of an education.

Cautious people are dull people. It's a big generalization and not for the cautious. Given a choice most people want to take the risky path in life that says 'Caution!' rather than the totally safe one. It's a human thing and it's the reason that one day the Nanny State will be hung from its own caution sign.

76

How to Clap

Clapping is how we communicate the feeling of uplift. Not surprisingly, it's very close to the sound pigeons make taking off. The higher you clap, the more you like something. Really brilliant things get standing ovations and everyone tries to clap above their head. The natural next step after a standing ovation would be to take off and fly. The lower you clap in front of your body, the less you appreciate something. Clapping below the waist is a good sign that you think something's absolute rubbish.

The people who clap loudest are generally those most frustrated at not getting the applause themselves. These clappers tend to over-perform and that's why you get a lot of appreciation-trumping; this starts with extra-loud clapping, then standing, followed by whooping and shouts of 'encore'. Underpants may get thrown at this stage. This can be embarrassing for the recipient, especially if they didn't believe the sermon was one of their best.

The British aren't very good at clapping and generally need to be encouraged to start. First clapper is a responsible role. He or she must decide whether applause is warranted and must also make a judgement that the symphony/play/speech is definitely over. The first clap is like a spark plug and it only takes a couple before the applause roars into life. Sometimes clapping misfires and only one or two people join in very briefly. This is worse than no clapping.

Polite clapping is a way of being very rude. It's when you just use the tips of your fingers to tap lightly against the opposing palm. It tells the performer that you're glad they've finished. Beefy clapping is when you use the fleshiest part of one hand to thump the other. This is manly clapping and is done when another man has hurt himself in the cause of sport.

An ancient puzzle in Zen Buddhism is to understand the sound of one hand clapping. It takes years of silent study to understand this conundrum. When you finally get it, don't expect a big round of applause. In the West, when you're caught with a glass of wine in your hand and need to do one-hand clapping, you can generally get away with slapping something else, like your leg or the face of a passing stranger.

How to Spectate

Most big stadiums have huge plasma screens that look like giant TVs. This is so you can get the authentic in-your-living-room experience when you're out. As most sports fans also have big TVs at home, you can get the authentic stadium experience by standing in your garden and watching the TV through the patio doors.

Some people spectate because they actually like opera or football. But the majority go to watch because other people go to watch too. As every kerbside con artist knows, the more people there are watching something, the more other people think there is something worth watching.

The difference between watching culture and watching sport is that culture has audiences and sport has crowds. You can get an opera crowd but you'll never get a football audience. That's because in culture it's the players that make the noise but in sport it's the crowd.

When you're spectating, binoculars are always handy.

They bring distant objects closer, but at the same time they make the idiot standing next to you seem further away. Beer goggles are also a great aid to the watching of sport, especially those with little intrinsic interest such as football. Indeed, American football watched sober makes no sense at all. Opera glasses, generally filled with gin and tonic, are the equivalent of beer goggles, which is why so many people enjoy the second half of an opera far more than the first.

The smell of fried onions on the breeze is the surest sign that you're at a great sporting event. Spectating is always enhanced by eating and drinking. Some opera festivals would be more accurately described as picnic festivals with background music. Roman emperors knew that the best way of keeping the populus happy was bread and games. The combination of the two was the origin of the hot dog.

All spectators want one day to be able to say of a great cultural/sporting moment 'I was there'. You don't need to add that at the precise moment the goal was scored/aria sung you were getting a hot dog or retrieving a rogue Malteser from under the chair in front.

There's a fine line between doing something spectacular and making a spectacle of yourself. People will happily watch both, but in future years you won't want to watch a recording of the latter.

How to Win

Fiercely competitive people are obsessed with winning and can turn a game of Scrabble into the Battle of Stalingrad. Equally tiresome at board games are the aggressively uncompetitive who embrace defeat at the earliest possible moment – it's their way of winning by not playing.

As the Swedish philosopher Björn Ulvaeus observed, 'The winner takes it all.' He also noted the Waterloo syndrome: 'I feel like I win when I lose.' Losing is actually more interesting than winning, which is why bookies are full of people gambling. Bizarrely, losing makes gamblers feel more alive. People who really like winning with their money spend a lot of time studying the form of their utility providers.

Losing in love is generally more emotionally enriching than winning in love. Good-looking people tend to be shallow because they've never had to overcome the colossal personal trauma of being refused a date.

The bigger the victory, the more it feels like a loss.

That's because you suddenly lose all the things that helped you win: purpose, determination and adrenalin. Lost causes are actually very popular because as long as there's never any chance of victory, you can happily soldier on content with the justice of your struggle.

One of the reasons lottery winners generally do so badly is that they've never had any experience of winning, and winning is a habit like anything else. Some people seem genetically predisposed to winning and some to losing, which is quite handy because it gives winners someone to beat and losers someone to blame.

Win-win solutions are very popular these days. This is an ideal outcome where everyone goes away feeling they have won something. This only works if people are playing the same game. When one person is playing poker and the other is playing snap, a win-win is highly unlikely.

Bad losers are people who get grumpy and aggressive when they lose. This is slightly odd as getting grumpy and aggressive seems an ideal way of losing. No one ever talks about a bad winner because winning is clearly enough.

The ideal behaviour is to win as though you've lost and lose as though you've won. It is possible to lose so well that the winner goes away thinking they've actually lost. This is an incredibly complex British approach to things which almost encourages people to lose so that they can win the battle to be the best loser. Other countries are happy to let us win this particular competition.

How to Ignore Stuff

There are two things in life that are difficult to ignore: world poverty and a jam doughnut. Of the two it's a lot easier to ignore world poverty. Virtually everything in life is shouting 'I am important, look at me'. The news thinks it's terribly important, which is why it has an important theme tune. But you can always ignore the news by saying 'No, that's not important to me', and then you can hum a happy tune instead.

When something unusual happens, the instinctive reaction is to gawp. For example, everyone knows what a car crash looks like but most people find it absolutely imperative to stop and stare. Indeed, the sight of someone not gawping at a car crash is in many ways more remarkable than the crash itself. Very few things in life are impossible to ignore. You can actually ignore death itself because once it succeeds in catching your eye, you're generally in no fit state to pay much attention.

The difference between an unpleasant person and an unpleasant bill is that the person will eventually go away if ignored. Ignoring people sounds rather passive but is actually the most violent way of treating someone short of actual confrontation. What you're doing in effect is denying they exist. It's a polite form of murder.

People who are really thick-skinned don't have to bother ignoring stuff because they don't notice it in the first place. It's sensitive people who have to make an effort to ignore unpleasant things. Often this unpleasant thing is a thick-skinned person. A great way of ignoring people is to unleash your inner call centre. You can then be permanently unavailable while giving the impression that you value people and will answer them shortly.

Ostriches are famous for burying their heads in the sand and hoping that predators will ignore them despite the fact that their colossal arses are clearly visible. The human equivalent of this is binning your post and hoping that no one will notice your massive overdraft.

The brain actually spends more energy ignoring what's irrelevant than it does focusing on what's relevant. That's why people who live near railways soon stop noticing the trains. It's a bit of a curse not to be able to ignore anything, and this can give rise to severe mental illness or, in the case above, trainspotting.

Meditation is simply a process of ignoring everything that usually demands attention. Eventually you get a great sense of inner peace. It might be what they mean when they say 'ignorance is bliss'. If it isn't, ignore me.

How to Brag

Braggers never brag about bragging. You won't hear many men saying, 'My molehills are more mountainous than yours.' However, you will hear men talking about bragging rights, especially in sport. These are like human rights in that the least deserving of them generally make the most of them.

Men automatically brag about three things: sporting achievement, sexual prowess and everything else. Interestingly, the fact that a man is rubbish at sport and pathetic in bed seems to having absolutely no bearing on his ability to brag. In fact bragging is often the one thing that he's really good at.

Women brag by reflection. They tend to construct conversations that reflect well on them so that other women can see the successful context in which they are modestly living. It's a more complex type of bragging and needs longer conversations. A man simply has to say he shags like a panther and then it's time for drinks all round.

Some people see their own life through a magnifying glass. Everything they say and do is spun into a silk purse of achievement. Eventually, they believe the hype and just become so marvellous that they float away on a cloud.

When you've done something really spectacular like beating the Pope at table tennis, it's difficult to slip into conversations without it sounding like bragging. Instead, you have to wait a lifetime for a conversation to arise about great sporting pontiffs.

One of the measures of whether a thing is worth doing is if you feel the need to brag about it. Bragging shows perhaps you didn't get as much out of it as you were hoping. People who do really dangerous or artistic or loving things often find it unnecessary to talk about them afterwards.

Actions speak louder than words but it's a close-run thing. We now live in a society where the talk-to-action ratio has been completely eroded. Talking about something is now as good as, and possibly more environmentally friendly than, doing something.

Bragging can be counterproductive. Saying you make the world's finest fairy cakes will have people secretly spitting them out into handy pot plants. Saying that your fairy cakes are rubbish will have people praising them to the skies and forcing them down even when they actually taste like pot plants. The British don't allow bragging unless they do it for you.

How to be Inconspicuous

Some people have a knack of drawing attention to themselves. In much the same way, others have a knack of drawing attention away from themselves. You probably know someone like this but can't bring them to mind.

In conversation it's easy to become virtually invisible. You can't just stay silent, otherwise people will notice how rude or shy you are. Instead, a mixture of 'Fair enough', 'I can't argue with that' and 'You're not wrong' will keep you immune from attention.

The truly inconspicuous aren't just low-impact in conversation when they're present. They also play virtually no part in conversation when they're absent. If you really don't want to be talked about, then all you have to do is be unswervingly nice. This will leave absolutely nothing whatsoever to say about you.

Hairstyles are important for the inconspicuous. Or rather, it's important not to have a recognizable style. For men the hairy-neck look is good, while with women anything that looks halfway between styles or colours is good. In both cases, what the look says is, 'I'm not worth it.'

For those who want to have a minimum impact socially, what you wear needs careful choosing. The basic rule is never to dress in a colour that couldn't be used in camouflage. Fashion goes through five phases: catwalk, boutique, high street, discount warehouse, jumble sale. The inconspicuous make their fashion move just as it arrives in the discount warehouse. Waiting for the jumble sale runs the risk of being inadvertently trendy.

The inconspicuous look as though they're wearing glasses even though they're not. That's because their natural focal length falls about two feet short of whatever it is they're looking at. Whatever the reverse of laser surgery is, they've had it.

The terminally inconspicuous always follow the two thirds rule. They are neither at the back nor at the front of anything. Neither are they in the middle, in case the middle suddenly turns into the central place to be. Instead, they are nestled safely in the front of the back or the back of the front.

How to be Cunning

The essence of cunning is thinking about the direction another person's heading and then digging a big hole along the route for them to fall into. It's an amusing hobby and explains why a lot of people enjoy it, however noble the pilgrimage of the other person. It's impossible to be cunning with someone who goes nowhere and does nothing, so the inert rarely suffer.

There is generally held to be a deceitful and manipulative element to cunning, but being considerate requires exactly the same mental processes but for nicer ends. You hear a lot about low cunning but very little about high cunning. That's because high cunning is perpetrated by people so above suspicion that you don't even notice it. Flattery is sugared cunning.

Cunning people and animals are generally portrayed as thin. Aesop doesn't have many fables about the cunning hippo. This has advantages for the larger person as no one suspects them of being crafty. The fox has a reputation for cunning but is actually not very bright. It just makes people who hunt feel better to claim they're after a four-legged Houdini. For the same reason fishermen often complain about fish being a bit slippery.

There are no evening classes in cunning. Lessons in cunning are learned the hard way. Crafty people aren't smarter than other people, they've just made more mistakes more often and can now avoid them. Young people are rarely cunning because they're still crashing through the pre-cunning disasters.

The cunning tend to assume other people are also cunning, and they start getting so clever and sly and devious they end up making bigger fools of themselves than those entirely without guile. The one weakness of cunning people is they think their cunning is invisible. It's not, especially if you're not very good at it. Then people regard you as if you were wearing a silly hat: if you want to look ridiculous with your machinations, that's your business.

In the past Cunning Folk were the wise men and women of rural communities who claimed to be able to help in affairs of the heart, health matters and witchcraft. They were much like modern-day therapists in that their main skill was being able to lead people into thinking about their own problems at a much more complex level than the initial problem warranted.

HOME HELP

How to Spill

Scientists have calculated that the gravitational pull between a cup of coffee and a white shirt is four times greater than normal. This is only exceeded by the pull between a chocolate éclair and a wedding dress. Furthermore, it is estimated by leading anthropologists that 5 per cent of all liquid ever prepared for internal consumption has been inadvertently applied externally.

Liquid has four natural states: resting, moving, spilling, staining. Every liquid, given the chance, will spill. It's the liquid's way of seeing if the grass is greener on the outside of its container. Never spill stain remover as this can leave an existential crisis on the carpet.

Slopping is the pre-tremor for spilling. You can slop your coffee on the way to your desk and congratulate yourself on the fact that you haven't spilt it but then discover that you've left a ring of brown water on your important document. The Olympic logo is living proof that its designer had five cups of coffee before cracking the final design.

Stains have an appalling reputation but to be fair they are only matter that's slightly lost. Why is raspberry jam on bread so much better than raspberry jam on shirt? The answer is probably because stains are billboard advertising that you're a clumsy half-wit.

Hotels encourage you to reuse your towels to save the environment. In a similar way, expensive restaurants should encourage diners to drink their wine from toddlers' sippy beakers so that table cloths don't have to be rewashed every evening.

Therapists advise us not to cry over spilt milk. This explains why dairy farmers find therapy incredibly frustrating. Spilling is actually perfectly natural. Nature is forever spilling stuff. Flooding, volcanic eruptions, tsunamis, avalanches are all sheer clumsiness on the part of nature. In fact, it's fair to say that the engine of evolution is the spilling of seed.

How to Clutter

Clutter is physical clatter. It's an overloading of physical space. Modern life is full of clutter: physical clutter, emotional clutter, e-clutter, information clutter and a host of other clutterages. Most kinds of mental and physical detoxing involve decluttering. Increased clutter is rarely prescribed for any affliction, although a bit more mental complexity is a good antidote to fundamentalism.

Teenagers and old people are both prone to clutter: with youth it's because their possessions have expanded into their living space, with old people because their living space has shrunk around their possessions. Tutankhamen's tomb looked like a typical teenager's bedroom and it's no coincidence that it remained undisturbed for 5,000 years as teens hate having any of their gear interfered with.

Nature is generally fairly cluttered and it's only because we live in a highly tended and organized landscape that we think otherwise. An ancient and unmanaged wood is an impenetrable cluttered mess much like virgin rainforest. That's why in fairy tales no one has picnics in the deep dark woods or, if they do, things end badly.

Nature may be cluttered but it's not disorganized. Similarly, a desk piled high with paperwork and other clutter is not necessarily the sign of an untidy mind. That person has brought back odd pieces of paper and files and old sandwich wrappers to build a protective and homely nest around themselves. As long as they don't also try and feed their team by regurgitation, they should be left in peace.

Most people have clutter. The important distinction is whether your clutter is in a neat filing system or whether your neat filing system is lost somewhere in the clutter. Some clutter is in itself a kind of organic filing system and its owner often claims they can locate anything needed within seconds. You should remind them that just because they can find it doesn't mean it hasn't started to decompose.

How to Clean

Cleaning is the penalty we pay for not living naked in the wilds. When you don't wash your hair, it starts to clean itself after a few weeks. When you don't clean your house for a few weeks, it looks like Tutankhamen's tomb.

One of the awful things about cleaning is that you can't start it until you've done tidying. And you can't do tidying until you've done sorting and you can't do that until you've got fundamental problems in your relationship ironed out or watched the football.

Men should be obliged by law to clean toilet bowls. Unbeknown to women, men never lift the seat as that would create a bigger target area and be less of a challenge. In fact sometimes we bounce up and down and shake things around just to make life more difficult. Naturally this sometimes causes accidents but they're difficult to spot in the dark.

Dust is the silent particulate presence of your mother-in-law in the house. Seeing dust anywhere gives you the sickening feeling that her finger will find it on her regular flying inspections. Dust, like poison, can be removed by sucking. Modern vacuum cleaners allow you to pick up all the dust from various rooms and then transfer it to your lungs, hair and clothing as you try to change the bag, bin, filter, etc.

Limescale is the waterborne equivalent of dust. Catalogues often show models in the shower delicately arranged to cover their naughty bits. If they were simply to have a quick shower in a hard-water area, they would be virtually invisible behind the screen because there would be more limestone in the shower than in the entire Peak District.

Cleaning solutions come in two flavours, lemon or pine. Why? No one knows. Never use the two together unless you want to end up with a surreal tropical pine forest smell. Really effective cleaning solutions remove fingerprints from all surfaces including your fingers.

Cleaners are divided into those who clean behind the fridge and those who sweep loose frozen peas under the fridge. Some people clean religiously to purge their inner demons and some people clean because they've lost a member of the family under a pile of junk. Some people use rubber gloves to clean the house. This is slightly eccentric because if you didn't use protective equipment to make the house filthy, why use it to clean the place up?

It's a great feeling when the cleaning is over and you can relax in a sparkling house. This is the moment you decide that if things ever got really bad, you could clean houses for a living. Or you decide that things have got really bad and you're going to get a cleaner.

How to Do Chores

For people with stressful lives, doing the chores can be a form of therapy. Spending an hour doing the laundry is a great way of forgetting all about your other worries unless of course you find a stranger's underpants in your washing machine.

Some people love chores. They make a little list of the things they have to do and then tick them off as they go, perhaps even timing themselves to see if they can break any records for efficiency. If you're one of these people, you need to get out more and not just to buy some more anti-bacterial bathroom gel.

About 12 per cent of the population live their entire life without ever doing any chores. These people either live lives of unimaginable squalor or they have a primary carer who waits on them hand and foot. Being a student is the difficult time where you lose your primary carer and begin to experiment with unimaginable squalor.

Men have traditionally been responsible for taking the rubbish out. This is generally at the request of the woman and represents her deep subliminal desire to get rid of the real rubbish, i.e. the man. For their part, men know that taking the rubbish out, done right, can involve an hour or so in the pub.

Vacuuming the house is a very quick way of sprucing it up simply because you can use the hoover to push everything out of the way. Cleaning an average-size room is also the exercise equivalent of ten minutes on the Nordic Skier, while changing the hoover bag is the mental equivalent of doing a Rubik's cube in a dust storm.

There is a time for everything in life and every so often the time comes round to don yellow rubber gloves for hand-to-hand combat with your vitreous china. Cleaning a toilet is good for the soul (as long as it is not being used by someone else at the time). Once you've done the toilet you know the worst is over. All that remains is to buff up the taps and you can have your coffee and biscuits. Make sure the last chore is washing your hands.

Chores are divided into daily (washing-up), weekly (bins) and once in a lifetime (cleaning behind the fridge). Doing the final category on a daily basis almost guarantees entry to a mental institution and, incidentally, explains why they are all so spotlessly clean inside.

How to be Safe

It's a dangerous world out there and safety should be our number one priority. Always take a few moments to familiarize yourself with the nearest emergency exits even when you are travelling by bicycle.

Nature is a born killer – ice, floods and volcanoes are a continual threat. Even a stiff wind can desiccate you like a coconut. These risks can be much reduced by telling people where you're going and wearing a reflective band.

Stalkers are another modern danger. The person on the other side of this book could have been following you around for years, going through your laundry and opening your letters (OK, they may be married to you but that's just a good cover).

Driving is incredibly dangerous as almost all deaths on the road involve a car. If you insist on driving, pre-inflate all airbags, wear a cycle helmet and drive defensively, preferably on the pavement. Whether you have a baby on board or not, have a sticker in the back window as these stickers can substantially reduce the impact of being rear-ended by a forty-ton truck.

In safety terms it is obviously extremely foolhardy to live on or anywhere near the edge. Life is like a platform – if you get too close to the edge, you're likely to be hit by someone opening their door. Stand well behind the yellow line of life or preferably in the designated waiting area. Ideally, wear a cycle helmet and adopt a brace position.

Normally you'd be better off staying at home were it not for the fact that most deaths occur in the home. Remember that water and electricity don't mix, so turn the lights off when you're in the bath and don't buy electricity from your water company. Wear a cycle helmet in the bath. The average garden shed is chock full of instruments of death. If you buy a lawnmower, insist on airbags, roll bars and side-impact protection. When mowing, wear a cycle helmet.

All domestic animals are stiff with rabies, tetanus and Lassa fever. Keep them under observation for six months before letting them into the house. Remember too that animals are essentially savage and, in the wild, a hamster is an attack animal. Before petting, wear a chain-mail/ biological warfare suit and cycle helmet.

One of the main risks to life these days is death. By taking a few sensible precautions this unnecessary risk can be avoided; check the nearest available exits, wear a cycle helmet and assume the brace position.

How to Deal with a Fly

Flies carry more than five times their body weight in pure irritation. A big part of this is their buzz. Flies buzz for the same reason that young men drive round with incredibly loud music in their car; they just want everyone to know that they are in your neighbourhood and ready to annoy you.

Millions of years of evolution have given flies the uncanny ability to wait quietly in your curtains until you sit down with a cup of tea. They then choose this exact moment to start playing head-butt the light shade.

The humane way to treat flies is to wait until they have shown themselves out of the room. You can wait until this happens and then they'll also have the remains of your decomposing body to feed on. It's also worth remembering that the reason the fly got in was because you opened the window to let the last one out.

Men suddenly revert to hunter-killer when faced with a fly, with rolled-up newspapers generally being the weapon of choice. Scientific experiments have shown that the

Daily Mail is the most effective as flies are often stunned by the paper long before being hit.

The Indiana Jones approach involves rolling up a tea towel and using it as a whip. The theory is that the tip of the whipped tea towel travels at the speed of light and therefore faster than a fly. Never mind that the fly has watched you spend half an hour rolling up the tea towel.

Fly paper is a sticky piece of paper which you hang in the centre of the room to attract flies. It makes an attractive centrepiece to any room and an interesting conversation point. Equally effective is chocolate cake, although you don't have to hang this up as flies will find it wherever you put it.

Flies literally have eyes in the back of their heads, so it's very difficult to sneak up on them. They can also process images seventeen times faster than your digital camera, so to a fly your lightning-fast newspaper strike appears to be moving at the speed of a narrow boat.

Interestingly, the one sure way of ridding a room of a buzzing fly is to imitate it by running around the room screaming. When you've finished, the fly will still be there but you'll now appreciate what fun they're having and let them get on with it.

How to Hide

There are two types of people in the world: those who are hiding and those who are seeking. At a deeper level, everyone who is hiding is hoping to be found and everyone who is seeking is looking for a place to hide. The secret to happiness must surely be for both hiders and seekers to stand in a well-lit room and talk to each other.

Hide-and-seek is a very popular game not because you're hiding but because someone is looking for you. There is also the darker fear that maybe no one is in fact looking for you at all. Very competitive people take hide-and-seek so seriously that they're sometimes never found. Which is actually a great way of getting rid of the over-competitive.

One of the benefits of hiding is that you can see people but they can't see you. Birdwatchers spend a lot of time in hides, which allow them to see birds. It means the rest of us can't see birdwatchers. So everyone wins.

Some women hide behind a thick layer of makeup. But underneath there is another woman struggling to get out with a smoother, more translucent layer of makeup. Men can hide behind a tough macho exterior. Strip away this exterior and there is often something softer underneath. Remember to ask for permission before you attempt to strip away the tough macho exterior.

There is a saying that if you are a tree, the best place to hide is in the woods. Tell that to the bit of tropical timber that now makes up your coffee table. Another popular saying is 'you can run but you can't hide'. For most people the opposite is true, that they can't run so they hide instead. Hiding is a stationary form of escape.

People like things to be hidden. A hidden agenda is much sexier than an agenda. People who have something to hide seem deeper than people who don't. That's why conspiracy theories are so popular. The fact that no one's ever found the Holy Grail is probably because it's not hidden.

Hiding is a form of power. I know where I am but you don't. That's why many inadequate people become voyeurs. Interestingly, when you cross a voyeur with an exhibitionist, you get a trainspotter, i.e. someone who stares at things in public.

There is something very glamorous about going into hiding. However, don't confuse this with letting someone give you a damn good hiding, which is different in important ways. Finally, remember that the best place to hide things is the same place you lose them because that's exactly the place you can't find them.

How to Borrow

Of begging, borrowing and stealing, borrowing does the most lasting psychological damage to the victim. You know the exact identity of the person who borrowed from you, you know that they've probably already passed the goods on to a third party and you know that the police simply won't be interested.

Frequent borrowers don't really think they're borrowing at all. Borrowing is simply their way of acquiring things. If you lend them something, they assume that you no longer want it. In their mind, you are a personal charity shop where second-hand goods can be picked up extremely cheaply.

However, not lending things can be as difficult as lending things. Telling someone they can't borrow something is like handing them a bad character reference. You have analysed everything you know about them and decided that, on balance, they are feckless, unreliable and with criminal tendencies.

Everyone who reads books has two libraries. At home they have the books they have read and that didn't make much impression, and then there are the books they really loved which they foolishly lent and are now on permanent display in their friends' bookcases.

Borrowing clothing is something done a lot by women. This is when they buy something to wear at a party, keep the receipt and then take it back the day after the party. Sometimes women borrow clothes from other women. In a way this is flattering because you clearly have nice clothes that people want to borrow. On the downside, people who borrow clothing tend to do something in it which involves stretching, fading and splattering it with unidentified muck.

Men don't borrow other men's clothing unless there is an imminent danger of hypothermia. Even noticing what another man is wearing is generally considered to be a step into the dark side of sexuality. On the other hand, men borrowing women's clothing is perfectly acceptable.

On the high street there are two main institutions for borrowing: the library and the bank. The difference is that you don't have to see the library manager to borrow a book. Also, when you return a book, you don't have to return a small brochure as an interest payment.

The acid test of a good neighbour is what you can borrow from them. A cup of sugar or a strimmer is perfectly acceptable, while borrowing a car, spouse or ride-on mower is really pushing the limits.

Borrowing money is a very tricky one. Some people will make sure they pay you back 8p while others think that £500 is not worth bothering about. To avoid this kind of awfulness, simply follow the motto: neither a borrower nor a lender be. Or, if you don't get your money back, borrow £500 worth of books back over the next ten years.

How to Measure

Measuring things is one of the greatest sources of unhappiness. Comparison always comes hard on the heels of measurement, and envy and bitterness follow on shortly afterwards. Some primitive tribes had a taboo on counting and they may well have been on to something.

Men know three measurements off by heart: how large their salary is, how long their penis is and how big the engine of their car is. Happiness for men is when salary over engine times penis equals twenty. Women are much more sensible and are more concerned with quality than quantity, except for shoes.

People tend to remember their vital measurements at different times in their life. For example, most people will remember what their waist measurement was when they were twenty-one and wonder for ever after why their trousers no longer fit.

Some people, especially at work, like to measure everything because this makes them feel as though they're in control. In reality, for everything that's accurately measured, there's some big and blobby unknown quantity lurking just round the corner.

Traditional imperial measures are based on understandable human measurements. For example, a yard was the length of a man's belt. It was also how far you could walk before you fell over after you'd taken your belt off. Similarly, a mile is 2,000 paces. When you try to count up to 2,000 paces, a kilometre is roughly where you get to by the time you forget what number you're on.

Most everyday objects are measured in feet, except for horses, which are measured in hands. Really large things are measured in double-decker buses, swimming pools or football pitches. For conversion purposes, a football pitch is 124 buses and a bus holds ⅛ of a swimming pool.

Minutes and hours are measured in 60s. The national speed limit and retirement age are also 60 or thereabouts. We used to work 60-hour weeks and retire at 60. Now the EU has reduced the working speed limit and we have to work 35 hours a week and retire at 70.

Very long distances are measured in light years. For example, it would take 30,000 light years to reach the edge of our galaxy. But long before that happened someone would accidentally turn the light off because they thought you weren't in the room.

How to Find Things

Things don't really get lost, they're just in the last place you left them. The reason you can't find them is because you've put them somewhere you don't usually leave them. For example, nobody in their right mind leaves the remote control on the fridge.

The good news is that once you start looking for it you'll spot it immediately because things that aren't where they're supposed to be stick out like a sore thumb. But that's only if you've left it on a surface. If it's got inside something like the bread bin, you won't be watching television until just after your next sandwich.

One of the most trying aspects of losing things is the advice you get from other people; for example, 'Where did you last have it?' If you knew where you last had it, you'd go and get it and it wouldn't be lost. Or people try to get all rigorous and say things like, 'Go through your last movements.' If you've gone back more than a year and you still haven't found anything, stop.

Normally the place you look in first is where the thing

is. But the difference is that instead of being on that place, it is now under that place. If you've lost something in the bedroom, it will be under the bed. Don't argue, just go and look.

When things get lost, people start looking in extraordinarily unlikely places. One moment you can't put your hands on the photo you had seconds ago, the next you're ripping out plasterwork, carpets and load-bearing walls. The reason for this is that the only thing you've really lost is the sensible part of your mind.

Lost things are always in exactly the same place: mobile phones are under the passenger seat of the car; your keys are in the pocket of your other jacket; your glasses are on the small table on top of that pile of books; the remote control is down the side of the sofa; and your illegitimate love-child is in Canada.

There is another category of things you often have to look for, and that is very small items that you drop accidentally. For women this is the fiddly bit at the back of an earring. For men it is the grub-screw that goes in the back of the boviator. The instinct is to freeze exactly where you are and to look at the floor directly beneath you. Don't bother. After falling from your fingers the clasp or screw or contact lens can actually move fifteen metres horizontally in any direction. It's going to be impossible to find so you should take the opportunity to forcibly remind yourself to stop being a loser.

ARGY-BARGY

How to Stay Calm

Calmness is a totally unnatural state. In a universe created by a big bang you wouldn't expect anything to be sitting quietly and nothing does. When you think you've found something tranquil, it's generally the calm before the storm. On the bright side, when you're in a storm, it's worth remembering that you're in the storm before the calm.

Taking a deep breath is always a good idea when you find yourself in a tight spot unless the tight spot happens to be underwater. A deep breath also keeps your lungs safely occupied at a time you're highly likely to say something you later regret.

Putting things in perspective always aids calmness. In artistic terms this means separating out the foreground from the background. In life, too, what's going on in the foreground may loom large for a moment but actually makes very little difference to the wider background.

Instead of having a panic button, it's much more useful to have a calm button which you press when things are getting stressful. Mentally reminding yourself that things could be worse helps. Unless of course things then do get worse. Even then you can remind yourself that everything eventually passes. This might mean that something even more awful is about to happen next but at least it gets you through the immediate crisis.

Interestingly, the path into meditative calm concentrates on breathing, which is a rhythm. It doesn't ask you to concentrate on something that's dead like the opposite wall. That's because rhythms are a lot more calming than silence: they are the reassuring background noise of the engine of the universe ticking over. It's when things get too calm and too quiet that you really need to worry.

Prescription drugs are often given to help people stay calm. Their effect is like the armoured glass in front of bank staff: transactions with the public seem calmer and safer and slightly removed from reality. A more natural recipe for calm is 'balm, palm and psalm' – that is, bath, massage and meditation, although this won't really help with road rage on the A34.

Some people are so unruffled and serene you get the sneaking suspicion that they don't actually understand anything that's happening around them because if they did they'd show more signs of life. Remember that still waters run deep but no one goes black-water rafting.

How to be Angry

There are two kinds of anger: the spoilt petulant truculence of someone who doesn't get their own way and your own righteous wrath at manifest and intolerable injustice.

People often get angry at what seems like the smallest thing. That's normally because they've recently suffered a big thing that surprised them before they could get angry. The small thing that comes after is the reminder of how angry they were at the big thing and they make up for lost time.

A fit of anger is much like a storm in that there's a tremendous amount of thunder and lightning. It's all very impressive while it lasts, but when it's all over, you realize that all that's happened is your tomato plant has fallen over. You can actually get much the same effect of anger by simply saying calmly, 'I am very, very angry.' This has the added benefit of not having to go to casualty because you've punched a wall.

Anger can be boiling righteous indignation at some appalling injustice but it is not always. You can be visiting your best friend in their charming country cottage when you strike your head forcefully on a low beam. Instantly you're hugely angry with the bloody beam, your stupid friend and their pathetic smelly little hovel.

When you're really angry, you blow your top. However, what goes up must come down. As your top begins to descend, you very quickly start to calculate where and how you're going to land safely. Most often this means slamming the door and storming into the garden/bedroom/pub.

Anger is one of the emotional big cats, and if you're going to be angry, it's important to do it properly. When you throw something, it's vital that it smashes with a satisfying crash. Throwing a powerball which then bounces round the room for half an hour will have more of a comic effect. Also it's very difficult to storm downstairs without breaking your neck. Make sure you're at the bottom of a flight of stairs and then storm upwards.

Being angry gives you a chance to swear. Remember to use filthy words that you don't normally use. Using phrases like 'Gordon Bennett!' and 'Dash it!' won't have the impact you desire. Once you're effing and blinding, you'll find that every other word is an expletive. Any more than that is gibbering and people will think less about pacifying you and more about sectioning you.

When you're angry, it's sometimes such a relief getting

everything off your chest that you feel an overwhelming desire to laugh and be affectionate afterwards. For the person at the receiving end this can be even more alarming than the anger.

How to Soothe

TLC is the anaesthetic for little emotional grazes and the way you apply it is by soothing. For women, soothing is easy, like falling off a log. Men are better at falling off logs.

Listening is the best soother. Get somebody to repeat their woes three times and they will seem rather unimportant, not just to you but to the person telling you. When listening, make sure you nod your head. But keep listening hard in case you suddenly have to shake your head. If in doubt just make small looping movements with your head until you know which way to go.

Saying the right things to people when you're soothing is very important. Once the person is in full flow, it's good to say you understand but don't say it too quickly, otherwise you'll give the impression you want them to shut up. An excellent rule is to say 'You must be...' followed by whatever emotion they're currently exhibiting. For little children you can also say 'there, there'. Don't confuse this with 'hear, hear', which is the way MPs show sexual arousal.

Ideally, take the upset person for a walk. Then make it longer and longer and longer. They'll suddenly realize they're miles from home and basic human needs such as food, warmth and shelter will quickly become more important than their petty emotional crisis.

British people find the physical component of soothing difficult. Traditionally any kind of touching is a prelude to full-blown intercourse, so suddenly giving someone a big hug can send very mixed messages. You can't go wrong with a swift double pat on the back. The general rule is that you can safely pat someone anywhere an American footballer wears protection apart from the crotch.

People are usually upset standing up, so a good soothing technique is to get them to sit down or even lie down. The closer you can get them to the horizontal the better. Clearly don't wrestle them to the ground if they're resistant but guide them to a chair and then recline it if that facility is available.

If sobbing is evident, whip out a handkerchief but make sure it's clean. A filthy one will not only upset the person further but will probably give them a nasty infection. Once they've finished and really messed the handkerchief up, tell them they can keep it. Or take it back if you think the overall gravity of the situation might call for DNA testing later.

How to Panic

Panic is paranoia with legs. Panicking is like pushing your fast-forward, delete and eject buttons all at once. The first thing that runs riot when you panic is your imagination. As imagination works at ten times the speed of common sense, your life suddenly seems to accelerate from plodding kitchen-sink drama to break-neck thriller.

Some people panic from birth and never really recover. Unless these people are on the verge of complete nervous breakdown, they don't seem to be able to generate any forward momentum in their lives. These people often serve as mobile panic inducers in other moderately apprehensive people.

Many people in life are calm on the outside but panicking quietly inside. Almost everybody occasionally has a panic attack. This is the realization that your entire life is actually a rickety scaffolding structure you've built very poorly without reference to the instructions and the whole thing is about to collapse.

Occasionally someone panics and then they very rapidly do exactly the right thing required by the situation. This is how medals are won and reputations acquired for having a cool head in a crisis.

Generally, the British don't do panic. Even when we're panic-buying, it all looks a lot more orderly than your average Italian supermarket. Mass panic is always a frightening phenomenon (especially at election time). In a crowd situation the trigger for setting off panic is somebody shouting in a loud, clear voice, 'Don't panic!!'

A panic button is a button you're supposed to press when panicking in order to summon help quickly. What happens in reality is you press the button and the help at the other end panics and that's the last you'll hear of them. It's called a panic button because clearly you can't be panicking if you're thinking straight enough to press it, but once you've pressed it and nothing happens, you really do start to panic.

There are two types of panicking: headless chicken and headlight rabbit. With the former you lose your head and then run around in all directions. With the latter you are transfixed by oncoming danger. Some people who seem to be caught in the headlights aren't panicking at all. Instead they're probably thinking, like the rabbit, that if the car doesn't slow down, it's going to be smashed to pieces.

How to Say No

A lot of trouble in life is the direct result of saying yes when you should have said no. It's an easy mistake to make, especially with some idiot kneeling directly in front of you with a ring in his hand.

Saying no is very difficult. The Japanese find it so difficult they don't even have a word for it. Instead they have degrees of yes which can mean anything from ecstatic acceptance to a hard slap in the face. On the other hand Americans love saying no. In fact they then ask you what part of no you don't understand. The honest answer is that you don't understand the bit that's not yes.

A good strategy is to say no as soon as anyone looks as though they're about to ask you something. It's then much easier to say 'I've already said no' when they tell you their ludicrous half-baked idea. Or, if it's a great idea, you can always beat a hasty retreat to yes. Never delay saying no. People will assume you agree with them until there is firm evidence to the contrary. An almost imperceptible lack of enthusiasm when you say yes really doesn't count as firm evidence of no.

You can upset people by saying no and it's generally a good idea to let them down gently. However, some people have a kind of internal bungee cord that means when you try to let them down, they just bounce straight back up. To make this kind understand no, you have to cut their cord, let them crash to earth and then bury them under ten feet of unequivocally negative concrete.

To make a no truly understood, it has to be said three times. The first is the most difficult. This is the one people can't quite believe you've said. When they start shouting or sobbing, you then have to say no again. Finally they realize you might actually mean no and then they try wheedling. One more no will finish them off and make you feel great. A successfully delivered no gives almost as much pleasure as receiving an unequivocal yes.

The reason why we say yes so often when we mean no is because more often than not we're ambushed. The person with the difficult question has been thinking about it for weeks, maybe years. They then want your answer immediately. The trick is to programme yourself to respond automatically, 'That's very interesting, I'll have to give that some serious thought.' But don't be dogmatic about this. There's no point saying it when the bus driver asks you if you want the next stop.

127

How to Disagree

In hotter countries disagreement is a kind of national sport. It's a bit like football without the ball: just people shouting at each for no good reason. In this country the most common way of disagreeing with someone is to say that you agree with them wholeheartedly and then make sure you never see them again for the rest of your life.

The British tend to avoid disagreeing with people in public in case our finely honed arguments are met with a finely honed knife. Instead we've developed the anti-disagreement phrase 'fair enough'. In longhand this means, 'If you want to believe that kind of rubbish and embarrass yourself every time you open your mouth, then good luck to you.'

One of the quickest ways of promoting disagreement is to start a sentence with the phrase 'I think you'll agree...'. Similarly, you can get almost instantaneous agreement by starting with 'I don't expect you to agree with this for one moment...'.

Disagreements are often over facts or things and who is in the possession of them. That's why Buddhists, who don't really do possessions, rarely disagree with anybody. Although this might also be because sitting cross-legged is probably the worst position to start a fight from.

Some people get real pleasure out of saying 'I completely disagree' after virtually any totally innocuous statement. This is a ploy so they can restart the conversation on their terms. It's like having the last word first.

A great way of saying that you disagree with someone is to say 'I don't disagree but...' or 'You're absolutely right but...'. In fact saying 'but' after anything is a clear indicator that you disagree; for example, 'Obviously Archie Gemill was the world's greatest footballer but...'.

Highly trained disagree-ers will use the word 'and' instead of 'but'. This gives the impression that they're simply building on your excellent first suggestion while adding a completely contrary and much more powerful suggestion of their own. Business people are trained to invite disagreement. After someone has told them that their idea is absolute pants, they'll say something like 'I welcome your challenge'. The real meaning of this is 'your career is over'.

It seems there is nothing in the world so small or insignificant that two human beings can't find a way of disagreeing about it. Although someone, somewhere will probably disagree.

How to Shout

Shouting is the conversational equivalent of getting physical. Real shoving often follows shortly afterwards, so shouting serves the same purpose as 'Caution, Vehicle Reversing!' – when you hear it, get out of the way.

Subordinate clauses are the first thing to go when you start shouting. Sentences get much shorter but their Anglo-Saxon content rapidly increases. Shouting generally arises from anger, frustration or uncertainty. That's why computers are the most shouted at things on earth. One day the nice woman in your satnav will be installed in the computer to calm things down.

The two most common occasions for shouting in modern life are when you have to ask a question to someone who's got their earphones in, and the second is when they reply without taking them out.

In general the volume of life is steadily increasing. There are few moments in the day when something isn't shouting at you, whether it's your alarm, radio, TV, telephone or boss. It's therefore not surprising that the first thing most people shout is 'Shut up!!!'

Shouting is often done to attract attention. In this country we have substituted queuing for shouting so everyone gets attention in turn without having to raise their voice. British shouters are therefore mad or violent. Evangelists who shout in public are therefore turning the public off in the quickest possible way. They are having precisely the same effect as trying to evangelize by queuing in Italy.

In Britain there's not much to shout about. One of the main attractions of football matches is you can shout like a wounded buffalo every time a man in shorts kicks a leather ball. It's not much of an excuse but surely a billion men worldwide can't be wrong.

Some people go through their whole life without shouting for fear that making too loud a noise would bring down all their mental plaster. It's actually good to shout once in a while, otherwise you lose the shouting muscle. Then, in an emergency, you find you can't shout for help and instead make ridiculous noises such as 'Cooee!!'

Shouting is in the same category of therapy as crying and orgasm in that it requires large intakes of breath to do properly. This largely explains why you can't do any of the above when swimming front crawl.

How to be Grumpy

Grumpiness is when grown-ups revert to being teenagers. It's a form of emotional strike action caused by refusal to accept the current offer on the table. If grumpiness could speak, it would be saying, 'I'm not happy because I'm not getting what I want.'

Unfortunately, one of the first signs of grumpiness is that communication ceases. Lips tighten, arms are crossed and doors are slammed. Often the only audible sign of a grump in progress is the long sigh. Grumpy sighs aren't little quiet things but are more akin to the release of pressurized air from the underside of a large steam engine. That's why you should never insert a whistle between the lips of the very grumpy.

The favourite pastime of the grumpy is to nitpick. If grumpy people choose to communicate, they will do this in the form of argument, in the teeth of reasonable common sense if need be. The acid test of grumpiness is whether you can say, 'Great, what a good idea.' It's impossible for the grumpy unless it's deep-fried in sarcasm.

When you are warned that someone is moody, you should be aware that this doesn't normally mean they are good moody. Moody generally means bad moody, in other words grumpy. The word 'grumpy' is the shortened version of Gorilla in Lumpy Sofa With Low Blood Sugar Level.

Grumpiness is mostly a male thing. It's a sign that says I want to be alone in my cave (preferably with my newspaper). Women find it more difficult to be grumpy simply because someone has to do the work while newspapers are being read in the cave. Women have moodiness, which can in turn trigger male grumpiness, often in the same office.

Some people are permanently grumpy. They have discovered that not being nice to anyone is actually an attractive lifestyle choice. People wouldn't stay grumpy if they weren't enjoying it. It's incredibly difficult to shift these people out of their grumpiness. You can pretend they're actually a little sunbeam underneath but this actually makes them even more grumpy.

The only way to deal with the deeply grumpy is to find everything they do or say incredibly funny. Most grumps are attention-seekers and hate not being taken seriously. Alternatively, treat them like teenagers and ask them to leave home at their earliest possible convenience.

How to Make Excuses

Excuses are the contraceptives of social life. They allow you to have a relationship with someone without anything too important developing. As with contraceptives, you only need to use one excuse at a time. Saying you're ill, having your hair done and going on holiday leaves the other person with the distinct impression that their dinner party is not an attractive prospect.

There is a strict hierarchy of excuses. It starts with headache, then tummy bug, appointments at dentists, doctors, hospital, then holiday, followed by funeral for colleague, loved one, oneself. 'I'm going to be on holiday' is an easy excuse but you then need to make a very big effort not to bump into that person when you're supposed to be in Corfu. 'I'm not feeling very well' is also pretty straightforward. The dangerous bit is when they ask you whether you're better and you clearly haven't a clue what they're talking about.

'I'm washing my hair' always sounds like the world's most pathetic excuse to a man. However, it's worth bearing in mind that women's hair washing is actually a major logistical operation on a par with washing the car, and for best results it's wise not to rush either.

Making excuses on the phone is an art, especially when trying to get rid of someone. Telephone calls from some people are like broadband in that they're always on. You can put the phone down, make a cup of tea, pick it up again and they'll still be wittering on. The best excuse is to pretend that there's someone at the door. You may even be forced to ring your own doorbell a couple of times. Just make sure you don't lock yourself out, otherwise you'll end up staying with the person you were trying to get rid of.

Rules are the best excuses. When someone asks you to go to the cinema, you can tell them your cast-iron rule that you only go to the cinema on Monday and (before they say it) you're doing your hair on Monday. Allergies are the excuse of the moment. If you don't want to go to the cinema, then let them know about your allergy to popcorn dust. If things get really desperate, you can say you've actually developed an allergy to them as a person.

In truth, all excuses are unnecessary. All you have to do is to say, 'No, thank you.' But remember that this upsets people much more than a pathetically weak excuse. The one thing people can't accept is that you don't actually want to do something they want to do. That's inexcusable.

How to Have a Secret

Secrets are secrets for two reasons. Either something nice is about to happen to somebody in the future or something unpleasant has happened to someone in the past. Then there are two kinds of secrets. The ones that you take to your grave and the ones that you take to your best friend.

Often people think they've done a marvellous job of keeping a secret because no one mentions it. In fact the opposite is probably true. When everyone guesses what's going on, no one thinks it's a secret and it's only when they casually mention it to you in conversation that you realize your big secret is actually common knowledge.

There are very few secrets about, which is why people love hearing them. Most people have two big secrets of their own, four 'secrets' that are really just embarrassing things they'd rather not talk about, and five secrets other people have told them.

All secrets have a tell-by date. This is the time between no one knowing and everyone knowing, where passing it on is still exciting. You'll know you've got the timing right when the pleasure of telling is more than the pain of betrayal. If it's your secret, you can only tell it once. The rest of the telling will then be done by the person you trusted never to tell. After all, if you've told them, it can't be much of a secret.

Being first into a secret is incredibly exciting. Being last is uncool and embarrassing. When someone rumbles your secret, the best defence is to be incredibly open: 'Slept with Brian? Of course, everybody knows that.' The nosey parker will quickly lose interest in your Brian lovefest if they think they're the last person to know and there's no one to tell.

The best way to keep a secret is to forget about it. Sadly the best way to betray a secret is to suddenly remember it when you're talking to a room full of people. A good way of winkling out secrets is to say to someone, 'Everyone knows your secret.' Any reaction other than 'what secret?' and you know you're onto something.

The secret service should be very secret but isn't. It should instead be run by the National Audit Office, who do all sorts of things no one's ever heard of. The trouble is secrets are interesting. They have a lot of energy attached to them and, like dogs, they want to get out.

Secret societies specialize in secrets that no one wants to hear. The more inane the secret, the more jealously guarded it is. Their most secret holy of holies is generally empty. Which is why they keep very quiet about it.

Natter and Chatter

How to Natter

The universe has a kind of background static called white noise. On earth this continual background noise is people having a natter. There's no clear message discernible in either but both can be quite comforting in their way.

For people who don't work in an office, having a natter is the equivalent of a meeting. There's usually an agenda to get through, some problem-solving brainstorming and appraisals of people who aren't at the meeting. Coffee and biscuits are often provided for extended natters. A good natter can take up to an hour and busy natterers can have back-to-back natters with different people all day. The more you natter, the more natterage you accumulate, which then has to be renattered.

Health issues are an absolute bedrock of nattering unless you're visiting someone in hospital. It's generally acceptable to admit to a minor ailment of your own against which you are fighting heroically, but when it comes to your partner's ailments you can really go to town with anatomical details that would make a surgeon blush. Older people nattering becomes a kind of internal organ recital.

Nattering sounds innocuous enough but it's a powerful way of spreading information though a community. If you have something important to communicate across a wide area, it's best just to have a quick natter with the head natterer in the area, or 'natterjack', as they are correctly known. Community support officers' main weapon in the fight against crime is the friendly natter (although if you're engaged in a really promising natter, you don't really want to be wearing a high-visibility jacket while doing so).

Nattering is a form of exercise for the elderly: it gets them out, gives them fresh air and provides an endorphin rush when they hear some particularly juicy gossip. Experienced natterers don't bother with the traditional talk-then-listen structure to a conversation. Instead, they both natter at the same time with bursts of intensity when the subject matter of their individual natterings coincides.

There are three ways to end nattering. The first is to say, 'I mustn't keep you.' This is said by the person who is tired of nattering to the person who shows no sign of tiring. You can also say, 'I must get on', as if you've suddenly remembered you're catching a flight. Finally you should always say, 'Mustn't grumble', even though you've been doing nothing else for the preceding hour and a half.

How to Have an Opinion

Some people seem to have opinions on everything. If you actually listen to them, you'll notice they normally have one big opinion that stretches a long way. People who really know about things also have opinions, but they can't be trusted because they're experts long divorced from common sense.

When it comes to people, you can have a very high opinion or a very low opinion of them. A very middle opinion of someone is a better thing to have because it simultaneously lowers your expectations of them and avoids disappointment in them.

About a third of all 'news' is lifted directly from surveys done by organizations that want to be in the news. These surveys are based on what a handful of people think but only people who have time to answer irritating questions. Therefore a large part of the news agenda is driven by the idle thoughts of idle people.

Surveys are always misrepresentative because they ask people their opinions. In reality people don't have opinions about things until they're asked for them. Then they'll give you the last opinion they've heard, which is someone else's opinion and very probably the result of another survey.

Having an opinion means you are no longer a 'don't know'. 'Don't knows' are divided into people who have never given something a moment's thought and those who've given it a huge amount of thought and are stumped by its inherent complexities. It would be a much better idea to have two separate boxes: 'Agonized indecision' and 'Don't give a monkey's chuff'.

In newspapers, opinion is free but facts are supposed to be sacred. On the internet the reverse is true: facts are free but opinion is sacred. As everyone has an opinion, the internet rarely comes up with a big opinion of its own. There will never be an internet prophet because online everyone is their own prophet, lawgiver and judge.

Differences of opinion are incredibly tiresome and are proof that the educational system has failed everyone except yourself. Opinions are incredibly hard to change because they are the vocal shoots of deep-rooted feelings. That's why rubbishing someone's opinion is a very quick way of hurting their feelings. On the other hand, telling someone they have every right to their opinion is really another way of saying that they have a right to be a total idiot.

How to be Self-Deprecating

Self-deprecation is a national sport in Britain and one that we're not very good at. The French have a reputation as great lovers because in every survey on the subject they always claim to be red hot, whereas any self-respecting British man would immediately claim to be absolutely rubbish, if not totally impotent.

Self-deprecation in love-making is actually a very sensible approach. If a man says to a woman she's likely to experience one minute of rubbish, then anything more will seem like an added bonus. And if you can only manage one minute of rubbish, then you can't be accused of over-promising.

Self-deprecation is a way of cutting yourself down to size. As our other national pastime is cutting other people down to size, self-deprecation saves your friends and family the time and trouble of doing it for you.

Habitual self-deprecators view any kind of praise as an assault with a deadly weapon. As a defence mechanism they often use counter-appreciation along the lines of 'you could have done it a thousand times better than me'. Beware of mistaking a simple statement of truth for self-deprecation. For example, the correct response to 'I'm never very good at night landings', announced over the tannoy, is not light laughter, it's immediately assuming the brace position.

Interestingly, when two self-deprecators meet, a game of inverse trumping starts where each person claims to be considerably worse than the other. This can lead to a rather tense and depressing atmosphere which can only be alleviated by someone else bouncing in and saying, 'You're both a lot better than me!'

Self-deprecation is verbal slapstick. When you say that you'll probably end up with the car on its roof, this is just a way of imagining the disastrous comic potential in any situation. It's even funnier when it actually happens.

You have to be careful using self-deprecation because there's always the danger that people will agree with you. When you've said, 'This dinner really isn't anything special', and your guest immediately starts scraping it into the bin, you'll know that your irony has passed unnoticed.

In life there is a limit to the nice things that can be said about you. When you say them all yourself, no one else will say them for you, but when you don't, then it's much more likely that other people will. If this fails, it might just be because you're not actually very nice. Which obviously you'd be the first to agree with.

How to Guess

L ife is a series of guesses. What makes it even more difficult is that there are no right answers. If guessing were easy, mind-readers would go out of business.

In the old style of education you either knew a fact or you didn't. Nowadays a lot of exams have multiple-choice questions, which means you leave school highly skilled in guesswork. But guesswork isn't as bad as it sounds because most of subsequent work life is also guesswork. Everyone guesses: estimating is how people with a trade guess; educated guesses are what professional people do; hopeless stabs in the dark are what statisticians do.

Guessing is done on the intake of breath because you're trying to draw information in, whilst facts are delivered on the outbreath because you are delivering reliable information into the world. Plumbers guess how long the job's going to take on the inbreath when they suck their teeth and tell you how much it's going to cost on the outbreath when you suck your teeth.

When someone asks you to guess something, this is

shorthand for 'I have finally found something which I know and I'm pretty confident you don't know'. This allows them a brief moment of superiority while you guess wrong. If you don't want to allow them even this simple pleasure, simple say 'I don't do guessing'. This will annoy them a gratifyingly large amount. You can also get an equal amount of pleasure by 'guessing' right because you actually know the right answer.

Often people will say, 'You'll never guess who I bumped into.' It's then actually a bit rude to make people guess if you've just said they'll never guess. On the other hand it sounds a bit rude to say 'You'll never guess so I'm going to tell you' because this makes you sound a bit thick and incapable of guessing. A good compromise is to give people three guesses, which allows them to triangulate: way too high, way too low, third way (also wrong).

There are all sorts of games based on guessing. Betting shops are basically guessing shops where you pay money to guess wrong. In the nation's boardrooms guessing is referred to as strategic thinking. Up and down the country many people enjoy organized guessing evenings otherwise referred to as pub quizzes.

Guesstimates are guesses that are supposed to be a little bit more accurate than just plain finger-in-the-air jobs. On the other hand estimesses are estimates that are totally and disastrously wrong and hence haven't caught on as much (outside major construction projects).

How to be Silent

Silence is the only time you can really hear yourself think. This largely explains the success of the iPod, which allows you to escape any dangerous exposure to silence. Keeping quiet is a dangerous and demanding thing to do as it brings you face to face with yourself. Many monks embrace this and make a vow of silence. Sadly this vow is not one that ever found its way into the marriage service.

Alligators have huge muscles that snap their jaws shut. Humans have similar huge muscles that keep their mouths open. It takes a massive effort for most people to keep their mouths shut, and if you look back over your life, most problems come from under-utilization of the alligator muscle. There is another added bonus to learning to keep your mouth shut and that is a much reduced incidence of obesity.

There are different types of silence. When you have someone drilling the road outside your bedroom, the silence when they stop is as loud as the drilling itself.

Embarrassing awkward silences and pregnant pauses have much more impact than what's said around them. A very good test of your relationship with someone is if you can sit comfortably with them in complete silence. Don't try this in interviews or on first dates.

In the same way that a man can't see a hole without looking down it, most people can't stand a silence without filling it. Some people feel a compulsive need to fill the silence with their own voice regardless of what it's saying. This wittering is a form of human white noise.

Silence is a powerful part of negotiation. Keep quiet long enough and people will knock themselves down and generally talk themselves into a very bad deal simply because they feel the need to say something to break the silence.

When you're used to silence, you begin to hear the noise quiet things make. For example, after a month in the country you begin to notice just what a racket photosynthesis makes. Similarly, once you learn to be silent you realize that your body is actually clanking away like an old plumbing system.

The great philosopher Wittgenstein once postulated that you can't think about something unless you can actually talk about it. He probably had many even more profound thoughts than this one but never found a way of expressing them.

How to Mollify

Mollification is a way of easing someone's pain shortly after you've caused it. Don't confuse mollifying with empathizing. The fact that you're having to mollify someone is generally a clear sign that you failed to empathize with them in the first place.

Never start mollification with 'Listen' or 'Look'. They've already seen and heard and clearly haven't liked either. Instead you must always start with 'You' followed rapidly by 'are so right' or, even better, 'should be angry given what's happened to you'. Immediate confirmation of their victim status is the first line of mollification.

Griping babies can be mollified by slinging them over your shoulder and patting their back. On no account try this with an adult. Similarly, late-night difficulties with a partner are unlikely to be soothed with a lullaby unless the argument is specifically about absence of lullabies in the relationship. When you're soothing ruffled feathers, it's very important to stroke the right way. Acknowledging that someone is upset is good but don't then put it down to their ridiculous hypersensitivity.

Physical comforting can aid mollification but use with care. No one wants to be hugged while they are still in the shouting stage of their displeasure. Hanging your head in shame is always good as it makes you look totally contrite and also makes it difficult for them to spot the smirk on your face.

A risky tactic in mollification is to try and prove that you hate yourself more than they hate you and for the same reason: you can't believe what a selfish stupid tactless idiot you are. You can then suggest that you might as well go and do something incredibly painful and humiliating to yourself. Make sure this is absurdly painful and quite impractical, otherwise they might agree.

How to be Silly

Being silly is doing something with no purpose on purpose. Silliness is what you have if you don't have common sense and it's equally common. The human being, once all its basic needs have been met, ascends into spirituality or descends into silliness. There is a middle way between silliness and religion, and this is known as amateur dramatics.

Silliness is a relative thing. One person's silliness is another's rank stupidity. One man's silly hat is another man's national costume. Nevertheless, there are quite a few people out there who have never been silly. This is very sad and they should be encouraged to join self-help groups where they all sit in a circle of chairs with whoopee cushions.

Being silly is a great way of combating stress. It's also a great way of causing stress. You should therefore only be silly with consenting adults. There's a big difference between people who are occasionally silly and people who are permanently silly. The latter can be very unpopular. Permanent silliness is a serious condition.

Clowns are people who are professionally silly and you would have thought that nothing could be sillier, except of course for the European regulations regarding safe levels of silliness in the profession. This shows that the people who take themselves most seriously end up doing the silliest things.

The best place to check for your silliness potential is in front of the mirror. If all you can see is a serious individual making his serious way in a serious world, you're either not very silly or you've mistaken a window for a mirror. Another quick test is to ask yourself when you last pulled a silly face. You might want to try it now unless you're on a train.

Being silly doesn't have to be done in a silly way. You can actually do it in a suit with a straight face. You'll then be known as an innovator and communicator. Or you'll be fired. Work is not generally welcoming of silliness, which is why very serious people in very serious meetings have to go to the loo for silliness breaks.

Children are naturally silly and the reason why adolescence is so difficult is because you have to replace silliness with coolness, which is even sillier but less natural. When an adult acts like a child, they are said to be silly. When a child acts like an adult, they are also told they're being silly. Silliness must therefore be about not acting your age whatever your age is. Research has shown that seventeen is the silliest age you can act unless you're seventeen, then it's fifteen.

How to be Serious

You hear of people having a silly streak but rarely of anyone having a serious streak. This is presumably because most people's natural resting state is serious rather than silly. Kings have jesters in tow, not the other way round, although nowadays celebrity jesters do come with very serious agents.

A serious situation is one where lives are threatened. This can be directly serious like lions at the bottom of your tree or indirectly serious like falling behind with your mortgage payments. Neither lions nor banks have a sense of humour, so being engagingly foolish won't improve matters with either.

People who take things seriously also tend to take themselves very seriously. Looked at seriously, the world is indeed a very serious place. It's perfectly possible to go your whole life without laughing. That's funny in itself but not to the person who's not laughing, as laughter shows insufficient respect for the gravity of life.

Work tends to be more serious than leisure, except for

professional sport, which is leisure taken very seriously. The business suit and the high-visibility jacket have one thing in common: they both say, 'Take me seriously.' Adding a hard hat to either says, 'I take seriousness very seriously indeed.'

Religious prophets also tend to take life seriously. You don't hear about any of them having a good laugh. To be fair, the Buddha smiles but that's a private joke. Politicians generally act on the belief that if you don't take yourself seriously, no one else will, although curiously the only politicians beloved by the people are the ones who take themselves quite lightly.

Pleasures come in two forms: serious and enjoyable. Classical music, opera and ballet tend to be serious pleasures, whereas darts and musicals are more enjoyable. Serious pleasures generally require government subsidy to survive, whilst enjoyable pleasures are taxed heavily by government, which gives you an interesting insight into who runs the government.

The Germans are quite wrongly said to have no sense of humour. What they have is a greater capacity for taking things seriously. Obviously, if you take the wrong thing seriously, this gets you into trouble, but it does work particularly well when applied to car manufacturing. In Britain taking things too seriously is a major sin. Sadly, we tend to take major infrastructure projects of national importance very lightly while making very heavy weather of obesity in dogs. It's a very serious situation. Seriously.

How to be Sensible

When asked to rate how sensible they are, sensible people usually give themselves a seven or eight out of ten. Nine or ten wouldn't be sensible. Sensibleness is quite a fragile thing. You can't have a competition to see who is the most sensible. That in itself wouldn't be sensible.

Sensible people prepare for a rainy day so intensely they often don't notice the sun is shining. Making a sensible decision often feels like a small defeat. Big personal and historical breakthroughs are seldom made through sensible decisions, but then again, neither are great catastrophes.

'He lived sensibly' is not a good thing to have on your headstone, unless it's a huge pink one. Living sensibly seems to involve not allowing your senses much life at all. Making love sensually is a lot better than making love sensibly, although married couples can be sensibly sensual so as not to wake the children.

Almost all actions are sensible to the person taking them at the time. Looking back, we can see that other acts would have been even more sensible. The Health and Safety industry is an attempt to force everyone to be sensible all the time. Like any industry, it's paid by results, meaning they encourage everyone to be ridiculously sensible, which is actually damaging to mental health and safety.

Having a sensible boyfriend or sensible girlfriend is like going out with a piece of non-slip carpet. It won't do you any harm but it's not going to be something that burns in the memory either. Childhood sweethearts who stay married for ever are generally suffering from premature sensibleness.

Sensible shoes are generally imagined to be flat-soled with a neat fastening. But if you want to wear shoes to impress your friends, make yourself feel better and attract a mate, wearing 'sensible' shoes is actually an act of complete madness.

Sensible people take a jumper, pay into a pension and keep their car tyres at the correct pressure. They also spend a lot of time worrying about foolish people who lack basic common sense. However, there's nothing you can do to make other people sensible. All you can do is to carry their jumper as well. But be careful. If you end up carrying seventeen jumpers, you may have inadvertently joined the ranks of the foolish.

How to Criticize

If all the world's a stage, then there must also be a hell of a lot of critics. Which means that every time you do or say anything in life, somebody else is mentally composing scathing reviews, none of which you'll ever read. The only two exceptions are the love letter and the P45, which are the two sincerest forms of criticism.

In life the ratio of people criticizing to people actually doing something is generally around ten to one. Many people see themselves as life management consultants; they are always available to tell you how to do virtually anything better than you're currently doing it. Often they're so busy with this valuable consultancy work that they don't have any time to do anything constructive themselves.

They say you shouldn't throw stones if you live in a glass house. But often the only way you find out that you're in a glass house is to throw stones and hear that shattering noise. That's the beginning of self-knowledge and the continual learning mechanism in any relationship.

Similarly they say, 'Let him who is without sin cast the first stone.' That's a nice thought but would mean virtual saints would hold back from criticizing out-and-out Nazis. Sometimes you've just got to put the pot-blacking and glass avoidance to one side and let rip with both barrels. If you're still worried about criticizing other people with a bit of mud-slinging, look on it as fertilizer for their personal growth.

Verbal criticism comes in two flavours, with comma and without comma: 'You've cut the grass too short' and 'You've cut the grass too short, you bloody idiot'. The first is the basis for a discussion, the second the high road to violence.

Giving criticism is almost as difficult as taking criticism. If you have the confidence to pull it off, a good way is to be harsh but fair. Harsh and unfair will just upset people, whereas fun and fair will come across less as criticism and more as a funfair.

Well-delivered criticism works on the basis that the offender (don't call them the offender obviously) has the very best of intentions but their chosen actions delivered precisely the opposite of the desired effect. If only the offender would change his actions, then everyone would achieve a higher and simultaneously deeper level of happiness and he would be able to avoid being such a bloody idiot.

Doing and Undoing

How to Volunteer

There are two types of volunteers: those with a heart swelling with passion and courage who step proudly forward knowing that the cause is just; and those who don't say 'no' fast enough. The number of people actively involved in voluntary activity on any particular weekend is vast, equivalent to our entire armed forces if slightly less destructive.

If you're afraid of volunteering, the golden rule is never attend an Annual General Meeting. These are meetings of voluntary groups which are theoretically open to the public and where wine/tea/biscuits are offered as a kind of honeytrap. At the AGM the six existing members of the group all sit on one side of the desk as if about to face the world's press. Any member of the public who comes through the door is automatically identified as a volunteer and possible future leader of the group.

Voluntary bodies are interested in three things: fundraising, recruitment and sexual abandon. The third isn't a stated interest but it's what most people think about in meetings. If it were to be an agenda item, the group might find recruitment and fundraising much easier.

Before going to any kind of voluntary meeting it's important to train yourself not to say, 'Well, if no one else will do it.' Uttering this phrase or anything similar is seen as evidence of unbridled enthusiasm for the job on offer.

You generally volunteer for something because you think you can run it better than the people currently running it. This can make for interesting committee meetings. Managing groups of volunteers can be difficult because of the 'you're lucky to have me' syndrome where people think they've done their bit just by turning up.

Leaving a voluntary organization is difficult. What you have to do is to give five year's notice that you're intending to stand down and then, once the five years have passed, agree to another five-year handover period so that a successor can be found.

Very, very occasionally some fresh-faced unspoilt individual arrives unannounced at a meeting and is very keen to get involved. For most, this is viewed in the same spirit as the arrival of a new messiah. For a few, such keenness has to be immediately put to the test by totally ignoring the new arrival and not asking their name for the next three meetings.

How to be Fair

Fairness is justice untainted by lawyers. It's a mixture of ordinary people's common sense and moral intuition and hence frightens the life out of political theorizers and philosophers of all persuasions. In general, people don't want everything, they just want fairness.

Revolutions often start with a thirst for fairness but end in things being even more unfair than when they started. Of course the English had their own revolution when they cut the king's head off. On reflection this didn't seem quite fair so we brought the monarchy back. A bit silly but it seemed fair at the time.

Fairness is extremely difficult to get in society and all sorts of different systems have tried and failed to deliver it. If only there were a way of applying 'you cut, I choose' at a national level. At the chocolate cake level this method applies absolute fairness to resource distribution while allowing for innate human fear and greed.

In commerce there is an old phrase, 'a fair exchange is no robbery'. Generally you only hear the person who's just made an absolute packet say this. The other person has been fleeced so badly that they are often speechless. They also say that all is fair in love and war. In reality quite the opposite is true. Nothing is fair in love or war, which is why the consequences of both can be so alarming. Interestingly, there is no equivalent to the Geneva Convention governing the rules of love.

The British have a worldwide reputation for fair play. In some parts of the world we had to force them into recognizing this but the message was finally hammered home. Nowadays a reputation for fair play often means a reputation for losing in a quite embarrassing way.

Fair play means you win without cheating. This gives the impression that you should wear Victorian-style trousers while playing sport and say sorry when someone stands on your face. Some people find this concept of fair play totally bewildering because for them cheating is just the most effective way of playing.

If fairness has a physical expression, it's a queue. A well-formed queue embodies the principle of 'first come, first served'. If you ever worry about how Britain would respond to a dictatorship, look at what happens to someone jumping a queue. It's the closest we ever get to a lynch mob. Continentals also embrace the 'first come, first served' principle but they have a mini-riot to work out who's first.

After 'mummy' and 'daddy' the first words children learn are 'it's not fair'. This is in fact extremely perceptive of them because all the evidence shows that life isn't at all fair. The trouble is, there just isn't enough fairness to go round.

How to Forget

It takes seven years to truly forget something. That's generally when you bump into someone at a party who you last saw seven years ago and who refreshes every gory detail. In truth, your mind remembers everything that's ever happened to you throughout the whole of your life. It's like certain images on your computer; you may think you've deleted them but they're still in there somewhere.

Trying to forget only makes you recall something more keenly. The trick is to remember something else when you think you might be remembering the thing you're trying to forget. Try linking a bad memory with lemon meringue pie. Eventually all you'll remember is the lemon meringue pie. You might also develop some kind of phobia about meringues but it's a risk worth taking.

Some people attempt to have a large number of exciting experiences when they're young so that they'll always have the memories when they're old. Sadly, when you get old you tend to forget trekking across Bhutan and instead remember in incredible detail the plug hole you had in your first kitchen sink.

The best way of not forgetting experiences in the future is to decide you're going to remember them properly when you have them. So you can either open all your senses and really imprint something indelibly on your heart and mind for ever or you can take a quick and instantly forgettable selfie.

There are two things in life you should never forget: passports and anniversaries. You're likely to need the former if you forget the latter. If you're forgetful, it's a good idea to write down everyone's birthdays and anniversaries in a little book. Remember to look at this book once in a while.

Occasionally you completely forget that you're supposed to be somewhere else for something incredibly important. In that sickening moment of remembering you suddenly have a fleeting glimpse of what it must be like in a parallel universe, where you're the same person but leading a completely different life to the one you're supposed to be living.

One thing worth remembering is that 'I forgot' is never a good excuse for anything. That's because everyone knows what you really mean is, 'It wasn't that important to me.' If it's really important, you'll remember. No one ever forgets their own birthday.

How to Undo Things

Without doubt the greatest innovation in computing is Ctrl+Z. Pressing these two little keys undoes what you've just done. If you keep pressing them, they keeping undoing things. It's like living life in reverse with the added thrill that you'll get things right next time. Real life has no such key. Nothing you've done can you undo. That's why many people choose the safe option of doing nothing. Opening your mouth is the equivalent of sending an email because there is no way of retrieving what's been said. Instead of being able to unsay what you've said, others tend to undo their relationship with you.

The Western way of doing things is progressive and we find undoing anything deeply counter-cultural. But if you work on the basis that everything carries the seeds of its own destruction, wilful deconstruction will inevitably lead to something new, so undoing is not so bad. Wrecking-ball operators are generally happy in their work.

Divorce is life's biggest undoing, aside from getting out of the insurance you didn't know you'd signed up for when you bought your new dishwasher. There's a Catch 22 in divorce. If it goes through smoothly and amicably, then you probably shouldn't have divorced, but if it's bitter, protracted and unpleasant, then you probably should have.

Undoing things is difficult but leaving things undone is equally troublesome. We tend to regret the things we haven't done more than the things we have, possibly because the unknown consequences of the former are more tantalizing than the mundane consequences of the latter.

The only way things that are done can be completely undone is by the total forgiveness of the person to whom the thing has been done. This means total surrender of the will of the perpetrator to the grace of the victim. Christianity's whole foundation is that Jesus Christ is a cosmic Ctrl+Z. Buddhism encourages you not to be idiotic in the first place.

Breast enlargements, like conservatories, are reversible but attempting either casts a shadow over your judgement in the first place. Good judgement often resides in deciding what doesn't need doing, buying, reading, seeing, learning, hearing, visiting, fixing or eating. And if they really do need doing, you can always undo your undoing.

How to Tinker

The rule with tinkering is if it ain't broke, fix it anyway. Men's preferred position for tinkering is to lie underneath something. This location most closely parallels the feeding-at-the-teat position and recalls feelings of comfort and security, if a little darker and oilier. New cars are tinkerproof. This means that male tinkering has migrated from shed to computer in recent years. The net result of this is that men's hands are cleaner but their minds are dirtier.

Tinkering happens in two distinct phases. The first is the unnecessary improvement idea, the purchase of vital tools and materials, the making of the tea, the donning of the soiled workwear, and the total demolition of the thing to be tinkered with. The second phase is the stopping for dinner, the losing interest, the watching TV and the going to bed.

Tinkerers shouldn't be confused with tinkers. Tinkers are door-to-door salesmen who earn money because people pay them to go from their door to someone else's door. As an added bonus you get a packet of dusters.

Tinkering for women comes in the form of gossip. Here certain facts are put on the workbench, pulled apart and then tinkered with to provide the most interesting emotional construct. This kind of tinkering can actually work without any facts at all, which is rather like a man tinkering with a car in an empty garage.

The enemy of tinkering is good design. No one spends much time tinkering with gloves because they fit perfectly, like the oft-mentioned hand in a glove. Incidentally, it's very difficult to tinker while wearing gloves, which may explain why Eskimos weren't at the forefront of the technological revolution.

Scientists like to pretend they are hard-faced marchers on the highway of scientific progress but in fact they're just professional tinkerers with cleaner workbenches. Most of the great scientific discoveries came through semi-idle men tinkering with things they shouldn't have been tinkering with. This gives lay tinkerers the excuse that if they could just have another hour alone in the shed, a Nobel Prize for Physics could be theirs.

Too much scientific tinkering can be extremely dangerous. We start by improving our DNA with a little tinkering and end up with another set of arms. Which, funnily enough, would actually be very useful for tinkering.

How to be a Hog

Hogging is the dark side of hugging. For example, hugging the duvet is fine but hogging the duvet absolutely isn't. A road hog is someone who won't let you in even though it makes absolutely no difference to their overall progress. A road hug is when someone flashes you and lets you in.

Hogging the bathroom is a very serious family problem. One person's quiet reflective reading time in the bathroom is another person's leg-crossing endurance test. Separate bathrooms are often the only thing that keeps a married couple together.

There's a new kind of hogging in the home called screenhogging. A screenhog is someone who spends far too long on the home computer doing totally unnecessary things when you want to get on and do your own totally unnecessary things.

Road hogs are anybody using the bit of road that you want to use. There are two kinds of road hog: those who drive too fast and cut you up, and those who drive too slow and have to be cut up for their own good.

In the acting world, the worst thing you can possibly hog is the limelight. This is because limelight is a very scarce resource in show business and a lot of people want to be in it. You don't find hogging where there's no scarcity, which is why laundry hogs are very rare.

In the computer world, memory-hogging files are ones that take up a lot of your available processing power. Humans also have memory-hogging files, which are memories you want to get rid of but can't (they also appear like pop-ups at odd times in an irritating way).

Hogging is taking more than your fair share of something and as such is deeply offensive to the British sense of fair play. That's why our motorways have signs which read 'Don't hog the middle lane'. To have the same effect in America the sign would read 'Slow Lane Free – Enjoy!!'

When someone hogs something, there's normally a little bit left for yourself. What you really have to look out for is someone who goes the whole hog. This is where they get everything and you end up with nothing. People who make a habit of doing this offend against natural justice, which is why you often end up with a communal hog roast.

How to be Incompetent

Scientists have discovered that much of the universe consists of dark matter, which does very little but provide drag on celestial objects. On earth we have a similar dark matter called incompetence, which also does very little apart from provide drag on important things you're trying to do quickly.

Incompetence is the dark space between two people where nothing happens. This space is called 'not my responsibility' and the way you travel through it is by being put through to another department. When you are on hold, you are in effect sitting in this dark space. Most people can't stand to be left there for more than a minute or so.

Incompetence can arise in the gap between two competent individuals, but where there is one or more incompetent individuals the gap of incompetence can sometimes be so wide as to be totally unbridgeable. Identifying the exact location of incompetence can be difficult in a large service organization, whereas this isn't the case in more traditional jobs like boat-building where a big hole is a bit of a giveaway.

In their own way incompetent people do manage to get things done: sadly this is normally the wrong thing, at the wrong time, in the wrong way, to the wrong people with the wrong piece of paper. Once upon a time this would have meant they were sacked. Now they just acquire a greater range of development needs and a glowing reference from their manager.

Competence has a gravitational pull, which is why competent busy people end up doing more and more and lazy incompetent people do less and less. The incompetent actually have a nice life because they seem to be surrounded by people who insist on doing things for themselves.

The incompetent have an incredible ability to prioritize the least important aspect of any job. Added to this they have the ability to make important documents hide under fridges. Finally they can be in continual communication with someone without ever mentioning the vital piece of life-saving information.

Competence in the old days used to mean the ability to light a fire and change a tyre. Now it is measured by your ability to remember your PIN, your password, your User ID, your national insurance number and your mother's maiden name. It's only after you've shown competence in all these that you can be transferred to someone in a different department who can't help you.

How to Procrastinate

Inertia sounds like the name of a newly privatized energy company. If it was, you wouldn't want to get your energy from them. In real life inertia is what stops things happening and it's the driving force behind procrastination.

Procrastination is vertical gravity. It is a powerful force that prevents us getting on with things. This force is particularly evident in beds, armchairs and offices, where it can keep things not happening for hours if not days. Entry-level procrastination is when you put off something today that you could quite easily do tomorrow. Advanced procrastination is when you put off the putting off until tomorrow.

For every reason to do something there are six reasons not to. Trying to think of the seventh is the seventh. In the workplace over half the cups of tea and coffee consumed in the average day are made instead of something more important being done. With meetings, roughly half are to avoid actual work being done. In fact, a good few jobs exist only to avoid life itself being lived.

Truly lazy people don't really count as procrastinators. They don't decide to put things off because they never really countenance putting them on in the first place. The terminally idle specifically avoid procrastination because it often involves a lot of displacement activity. Certain hard-core procrastinators will expend far more energy on their various displacement activities than the initial job involved.

In business they have a great excuse for procrastination called 'just in time management', where things are done at the last moment to save cost. In real life this is called 'close shave management', where things are done at the last moment to avert total catastrophe. This approach is surprisingly popular as many people need a scary deadline to kick-start themselves. Doing things in a last-minute panic is fine if you've enjoyed all the time you've wasted beforehand. With procrastination you don't get any enjoyment, just a kind of unpleasant slow-rising panic.

Procrastination can be thought of as a valid health and safety measure. After all it's only fools who rush in. You may look as though you're slumped in an armchair like a sack of potatoes, but in fact you're carrying out a vital risk assessment of your forthcoming burst of activity.

How to Finish

Current research, in the process of being completed, shows that the proportion of things started in life to things finished is eighteen to one. Starting is easy because you don't know the difficulties and you're still heady with the whiff of good intentions. You then rapidly hit the difficult phase, which can only be overcome by the hard-work phase. The easiest way to get round these two insurmountable difficulties is to start something else.

They say a job isn't finished until the paperwork is done (this is especially the case in the wallpaper-hanging trade). Actually the job isn't properly finished until the money is in the bank (except, ironically, for banks, who get the money and then do the paperwork). Many businesses go under because they do the work but can't be bothered to invoice for it. They are great people to do free work for you as long as you can get them round before they go bust.

Having the end of any project in sight immediately reduces your concentration levels by 90 per cent. This is when you're most likely to ice 'Happy Birthday' on your seven-tier wedding cake. Some people can never finish anything because they are perfectionists and there's always another microscopic adjustment to be made. The only way they'll ever finish is if they're physically removed from the task and held captive while their project is removed from the building.

In life there are as many false finishes as there are false starts. That's because life is one thing after another and it's almost impossible to finish anything cleanly. When things do finish, the three things that generally start immediately are nostalgia, regret and totally inaccurate myths.

Children are always very keen to be first at finishing things. This tends to wear off later in life when the great finishing line of death gets closer. The interesting thing about life in general is that it's definitely a race but no one knows where the finish line is. That's why it's so difficult to decide how quickly to run. Life in general has a great way of finishing things by bringing them full circle so that things start and finish at the same time and often in the same place. So if you're wondering where it's all going to end, just look at where it all began. All bus routes end in the depot.

FUNCTIONAL BODIES

How to Have a Body

The body is a mobile home for the brain. Like a mobile home, it is a self-sufficient unit that only needs a bit of fuel to keep it going for years. The only difference is that mobile homes don't reproduce, thank God.

The only unnatural body shapes are the ones you get in the fashion industry. These are made in the same way as *foie gras* only in reverse: instead of force-feeding they are force-starved. The result is supposed to be tasty, but when you know how it's achieved, it makes you feel a bit ill.

Everyone's body looks either like a fruit or a vegetable. Most men aspire to the parsnip look, preferably with the thick bit at the top. Body-builders tend to overdo it and end up more like a turnip. The average man starts as a carrot and ends up as a potato. Women generally aspire to the butternut squash look (it looks better than it sounds), but with age things tend to go pear-shaped. Remember, whatever fruit or veg you resemble, for someone you're the ideal five portions.

No one has a perfect body but everyone has a little bit of their body of which they're quietly proud. When you've got a good nose, you tend to have a mental image of yourself as a fine-looking nose with some other bits and pieces attached. If other people notice your best bit and agree and point out how fine it is, for some reason you automatically like them.

Sex is a bodily function and the body is covered in erogenous zones. If you want to know which bits are erogenous, run your hands over your naked body until something feels good or you're expelled from the library. Interestingly, most erogenous zones come in pairs: buttocks, breasts, feet, eyes, twins, etc. It's very unusual to find someone who expresses a preference for a right buttock or a left breast. Making love to such a person tends to be a rather one-sided affair.

The body is an amazing thing and is capable of incredible feats of athleticism, gymnastics and endurance. Fortunately it also has an override system called the brain. As you get older, your body starts to deteriorate. Sadly, you can't trade it in for a new one, although part exchange is now an option.

186

How to Whistle

Whistling is the sound of jauntiness leaking out of your body. People who walk around whistling are like human ice-cream vans advertising the good things inside them with a merry tune. They are also assumed to be two sandwiches short of a picnic.

It's impossible to be depressed when you're whistling but it's very easy to depress other people. Tuneless whistling is an audible sign that the whistler's brain is idling in neutral. It's also the sound you're left with if you remove chewing gum from the kind of person who chews gum.

You can measure job satisfaction by the amount of whistling you do while you work. Not surprisingly, it's difficult to imagine a whistling lawyer. Builders are famous for whistling. When a woman passes a building site, they will often whistle at her to draw attention to the quality of their brickwork, concrete pouring, etc.

Men seem to be better at whistling than women. That's because men have a deeper fascination with their bodies as musical instruments. When the young woman is developing her social skills, the young man will be seeing what noises he can emit from various holes in his body. A powerful whistle is one of those things that every man is quietly very pleased to own. However, at crucial moments like hailing a taxi, men can suffer from embarrassing whistle dysfunction, when it comes out as a feeble blowing sound.

There are many different whistles. The simple lip whistle is where you arrange your mouth round an invisible straw and then blow rather than suck. Advanced whistling is done with two fingers in the mouth and can direct a sheep dog at half a mile. The Tibetan six-fingered whistle can drop a yak at a hundred paces.

Whistling is the lowest form of music. Even humming is better because you can pretend you're actually singing but don't know the words. You'll notice that there is precious little whistling in classical opera. Wagner's epic Ring Cycle has absolutely no whistling and is much the poorer for it. If there were a minor character who came on and whistled for a bit, the Twilight of the Gods wouldn't seem such a big deal.

How to Look

Everyone sees but few look. For most people, 'having a good look' only happens when something interests them. For the small minority who are in permanent 'have a good look' mode, everything is interesting. In general, the more you look at something, the more interesting it becomes.

On average we see a thousand advertising messages a day. When we go to bed, we might remember one of them. That tells us two things: most advertising is wasted and just because we've got our eyes open doesn't mean we're looking.

The song says that you can look but you better not touch. But looking is a way of touching, which is why you can often sense when you're being looked at. Similarly, when you look into some individual's eyes, it gives you a physical jolt as if you'd been kicked by a small horse.

Many people don't look much because what's happening inside their head is far more interesting. The less they look at the real world, the more unreal their internal world becomes. The level of people's eyes is a good indicator of where their minds are: eyes up, daydreamer; eyes ahead, well-adjusted person; eyes down, introvert or bingo player.

Love is blind but has a great sense of touch. More interesting than love at first sight is love at seventy-fourth sight, when someone who was part of your comfortable visual furniture suddenly becomes a thing of incredible beauty. The world would be a much better place if we could see everyone as incredibly beautiful but that would make falling in love a lot less special.

Just because you're looking at something carefully doesn't mean you can see it properly. That's because everyone wears the distorting glasses of their personality: paranoid people see everything as a conspiracy, greedy people see everything as a potential profit or snack. The rule is you don't see the world as it is, but as you are.

People only see what they want to see. Being something or someone that no one wants to see is therefore the closest we're likely to get to being invisible. Advanced physicists and philosophers will tell you that things only exist when you look at them. It would therefore be a great experiment if everyone agreed not to look at advanced physicists and philosophers for a while.

How to Blow

A blow is anything that takes the wind out of you and directs it somewhere else. Interestingly, a blow to the head isn't as soft and erotic as it sounds. A body blow sounds like a very trendy form of spa therapy but in reality makes you feel a lot worse than when you started.

Children's text books often talk about how each lung has the surface area of Wembley Stadium. This seems rather impressive but doesn't seem to make much difference when it comes to blowing up children's balloons, which seem to require fifteen lungfuls applied at the same force as a jet engine. On that note it would be rather nice if, when being breathalysed by the police, they inflated a balloon that said on it, 'You're nicked.'

The blow job is not, as some sheltered people assume, a kiss blown from the hand. In fact the blow job is a complete misnomer, potentially as dangerous as calling a blowpipe a suckpipe. If blowing was really required, then the casualty wards would be full of men in various states of carnal engagement with leaf blowers rather than vacuum cleaners.

Compared to a surfacing blue whale, the average human blow is a sorry affair. It has been calculated that you only have to be about thirty before you need two breaths to extinguish the candles on your birthday cake. A blue whale 3,000 years old would still have no trouble with its cake.

Halfway between blowing your candles out and dealing someone a blow is blowing your top. This is when pent-up forces escape from all orifices in your head; it generally starts with steam emitting from the ears and nose, followed by something exceptionally rude and loud escaping from the mouth.

In the old days when the British weren't allowed to express any kind of emotion, blowing one's top was done through one's pipe, which puffed like the *Flying Scotsman* leaving King's Cross with a particularly long train. Nowadays the equivalent release of pressure in the head is the removal of the earplugs of the iPod.

Blowing is actually quite healthy as it clears the lungs completely and encourages you to refill them with fresh air. That's why brass bands generally play happy music whilst string quartets slumped over their instruments don't. Whistling is the equivalent of playing in your own brass band while whinging is the personal viola.

How to Pick

One of the disadvantages of being cloven-hoofed is that you can't pick your nose. Primates have fingers and thumbs and are therefore equipped with all the tools you need to pick at yourself, other people and other things that are a little bit loose and could do with removing.

Monkeys decided that picking themselves and each other was just about as much fun as evolution had to offer and called it a day. *Homo sapiens*, on the other hand, decided to use its fingers to build advanced civilizations and leave picking as a leisure activity for the sofa and car. It's difficult to know which species made the right decision.

The reward for picking is smoothness: scabs, mucus, spots all need to be removed to keep things nice and smooth. However, picking holes in something already smooth can be equally satisfying and is one of the main functions of committees.

Picking things is clearly a nervous activity. Ironically, so is nail-biting which, done to extreme, completely rules out the possibility of picking. If you're a naturally nervous person, you have to make a choice early on in life whether to be a biter or a picker.

Nail-biters obviously can't pick off labels. It's worth remembering that if you can't pick off a price tag, people will know how much you've spent on them, your relationships will be irreparably damaged and you will end up with nothing but your nails for company. Chew on that.

For people with nails, label-picking happens in three stages: the first is when you start picking at one corner to give yourself a little flap to hold onto; the second phase is when you try and peel back the flap; the third phase is when the glossy top of the label separates from its barnacle-like bottom. Once you start to see the white understreaks of a label, you then have two options. You can either just keep ripping away merrily and then spend the next hour chiselling away at the understreaks. Alternatively, you can try picking at another corner to give yourself a better flap to pull on. If you've tried four corners and you're still getting nowhere, revert to route one.

Fortunately, some packages now have 'peel here' labels that allow you to lift off the label painlessly. Generally these labels are found on packaging that requires a blowtorch and an ice-pick to get open.

How to Lick

The modern tongue is virtually a prisoner in the mouth. That's why sticking your tongue out is very rude but also rather saucy: it's a kind of entry-level flashing. Tongues are extremely sensitive and can determine thousands of different flavours including the three used in traditional British cooking.

What food, sex and envelopes used to have in common was that they all involved licking. With self-seal envelopes we are now down to just food and sex, which is a shame because licking a letter before you sent it added an interesting sensual angle to your correspondence with the tax authorities. Self-adhesive stamps have added to the precipitous decline in licking. To be fair, they do make sending your Christmas cards easier because licking eighty stamps was an absolute nightmare unless you had a handy Labrador or French boyfriend.

One of the main attractions of ice cream is that you can lick it. People who eat ice cream with their teeth and chew it are slightly missing the point. An excellent training aid for licking is the jam doughnut, as it's impossible to eat one without licking your lips and fingers afterwards. Some people cheat and lick the sugar off first, but then the doughnut ends up looking like a hairless Chihuahua and is most unappetizing.

Licking has no place socially and the rule is never lick a person you haven't already kissed on the lips. Similarly, never lick somebody in the office unless you are on an advanced team-building course. Licking people reveals the wide range of flavours they come in: there's sweet, salty, cheesy, BBQ and prawn cocktail. Or, if they've had a bath recently, mango, pomegranate, seaweed and strawberry. That's why licking someone straight after a bath is the equivalent of one portion of fruit and veg.

Before wet wipes, the tongue acted as a mobile cleaning unit. The tongue would be applied to a hanky and the hanky applied to the mess/baby/wound. Even now, a thorough beauty regime can be carried out using nothing more than finger and tongue. Licking is still very important in love-making but you should use moderation. Attempting to lick someone's entire back, for example, especially if they're a large person, will just make you dehydrated and make the recipient feel like you're doing some kind of minor paint job.

How to Sit

In the old days workers were divided into blue collar and white collar. Nowadays workers are divided into those who work standing up and those who work sitting down. Interestingly, when workers strike, they make a big effort not to sit down. Instead they stand in picket lines because sitting down would imply that they were too lazy to work in the first place. Only students do sit-ins, but in their case this is more active than what they normally do, which is lie-ins.

Sitting is generally recognized to be the halfway state between waking and sleeping. That's why you don't have chairs in your kitchen or bedroom. Chairs are for waiting rooms, sitting rooms and meeting rooms. In all of these no real work takes place.

Children are expert sitters, possibly because they have a much closer relationship with the ground. Some adults also sit on the floor. These adults view chairs as instruments of capitalist oppression and like to sit cross-legged on the floor to show how grounded and environmentally friendly they are. Theoretically they could travel as cargo on aeroplanes because they don't need a seat but they never seem to volunteer for this.

How you sit on a chair tells the world all about your sexuality. Men who sit with their legs wide apart are generally airing their dominant organ. These men also tend to sit low in the chair as if to suggest that the sheer weight of their genitalia is dragging them downwards.

At the other end of the spectrum are men who cross their legs above their knee and point their toes. This signifies that they are very at home with their feminine side or they are desperate for the loo. The fact that women often sit cross-legged may be an evolutionary response to an inadequate supply of ladies' conveniences.

Nervous people never make contact with the back of a chair. Instead they sit on chairs like birds sit on perches, i.e. they perch. When you suggest they sit back, they move an inch backwards and lean even further forward to compensate. Sometimes you have to manhandle them into the cushions to get them to relax.

When faced with an armchair, a significant proportion of people put their legs over the arms. In a sofa they may even put their legs over the backrest. This is a primitive wombing reflex with only the umbilical remote control and mobile phone to link them to the outside world. Old people often have special chairs that tilt and rock. These are basically flight simulators and let old people have slow-motion rollercoaster rides when you're not looking.

How to Squeeze

A squeeze is a temporary squash. It's also a lot more upmarket. Squeezed orange juice is approximately ten times more expensive than orange squash. The best things to squeeze are those things that are relatively hard on the outside but soft on the inside such as lemons, chocolate éclairs and grandmas.

Humans like squeezing. A handshake is basically a hand squeeze whilst a hug is a full-body squeeze. Kissing involves squeezing your lips and squashing them against someone else's lips. About a third of love-making consists of squeezing, which is roughly the same proportion as in washing-up with a sponge.

Being squeezed can be quite pleasurable as it reminds you of where all your vital bits are. A recession is an economic squeeze and can also be quite refreshing by reminding you of what's really important. But squeezing has to stop short of crushing, where your outsides start to impinge on your insides.

The world is divided into those who squeeze the toothpaste in the middle in a wanton act of self-indulgence and those who, for the greater long-term good of the community, squeeze at the bottom. When these two types live together, it means that the latter decent people have to continually remodel and plump up the toothpaste so that selfish hedonists can once more squeeze the seductively engorged area.

One of the reasons no one smiles on the London Underground is that they have all undergone the surreal trauma of being squeezed back into a tube. In general squeezing has to be done voluntarily, otherwise it's an invasion of body space and feels a lot like squashing. Boa constrictors kill their prey by squeezing the life out of them. They're like chat-show hosts who don't know when to stop.

How to be Clumsy

Clum is the invisible sticky matter in the universe that makes things go wrong. It is left over from the big bang, which was the first colossal act of clumsiness. Things only go smoothly in life when there is very little clum around. Sadly the world is packed full of clum and the resulting clumsiness, which explains why plans, hearts and favourite jugs regularly get broken.

You might have thought that human clumsiness would have been bred out by evolution. Far from it: clumsiness is actually a great way of meeting new people and apologizing profusely to them. In fact the whole of evolution is one clumsy mistake after another. Nature itself is spectacularly clumsy and rarely a day goes by without volcanic eruptions, massive earthquakes and comets crashing into planets.

Clumsy people are ever so slightly at odds with their environment; they move like learner drivers drive without, however, a big red C plate to let us know they're coming. However, the clumsy never believe themselves to be clumsy. To them it seems like there is a grand conspiracy of things, led by delicate porcelain figurines, to jostle them and provoke a physical confrontation.

Not surprisingly, going out with a clumsy person is a great way of reducing your dependence on material things. The thing clumsy people are most likely to whisper in your ear during love-making is 'sorry'. There's also a good chance they will head-butt you as they do this.

Clumsiness is a three-stage process: the first is the act of destruction; this is followed by the swearing stage or apology stage (depending on who else is involved); finally there is the clearing-up and restoration stage, which in itself often leads straight back to stage one.

Most people feel quite warmly towards the clumsy, unless you're the person being accidentally barged into the swimming pool. Perhaps it's because their exterior clumsiness is an outward and physical manifestation of the internal awkwardness everyone feels in the China Shop of life.

Clumsiness is the enemy of gracefulness. A swan is grace in motion but not when it tries to land on ice. Slapstick comedy is based on rampant clumsiness. That's why classical ballet is an art and pantomime isn't; it's also why one of the funniest things on earth is when you see a line of ballet dancers fall into an orchestra pit.

HEART AND SOUL

How to Wish

When you wish on an astral body, the first choice is usually a star. That's because it's impossibly remote. No one wishes on the moon because it's a little too human, coming and going and generally being a bit moody.

If you see lots of falling stars, you soon run out of things to wish for – after paying the mortgage, ensuring the health of your loved ones and delivering world peace. Once you're down to wishing the inside of your oven clean, you might as well do the job yourself.

A wishing well is a popular place for people to make wishes. Once upon a time the person who owned the well must have wished that people would throw money in it for no reason. You can imagine how impressed he is now.

Inside every Christmas turkey, there's a wishbone. To get it you have to kill, cook and eat the turkey, which, to be honest, were probably not the turkey's big three wishes. If you then make a wish for a small plastic puzzle and paper hat, there's every chance it will be granted.

Many people who scoff at the power of prayer are happy to believe in the power of curses. Curses are wishes for bad things to happen, generally to other people. It's not a nice thing to do but most of us carry around a little collection of mental voodoo dolls to use as pincushions. On the basis that you get what you give in life, it's probably a better bet to be a fairy godmother removing other people's pins.

They say that you should be careful what you wish for in case you get it. 'They' might have got this slightly wrong. The alternative is to wish for something you don't want and then get it, so on balance it's probably worth asking for the good stuff in the first place.

Counting your blessings is a way of reminding yourself that many aspects of your own life are a wish come true for other people in worse circumstances. Therapists often say that wishing is a form of positive visualization that goes a long way to making your desires a reality.

Lots of people do wishful thinking, which is a way of making the world seem better. Much rarer is wishful acting, where you choose to make the world a better place. If you want to try this, simply convert your Wish List into a To Do list.

How to be Bored

'I am bored' means 'I am boring', because the only thing that can truly bore you is yourself. Even crashing bores can be quite interesting if you take a slightly detached interest in just how boring that person can get without losing their own will to live. The more interesting you find someone, the more interesting they become.

Doing nothing doesn't have to be boring. You can do a huge amount of nothing and be completely absorbed: this indeed is the basis of all philosophy. On the other hand the more you look for instant gratification, the more bored you will become.

Being bored with everything is often seen as a pretty cool state of mind and seventeen-year-olds specialize in a terrible world-weariness that comes from having spent seventeen long years on the earth, much of it in bus stops. What you find a little later is that it's the state of being cool that's the really boring place to be.

Boredom is the great luxury of the developed world. Like most luxuries, the more you have of it, the less you like it. Most nasty things come from boredom: devil worship, vandalism and daytime TV. Lack of contrast in anything leads directly to boredom. Food is not boring if you're hungry, work is fascinating when you're poor and sex is totally mesmerizing when you don't have it.

Boredom is the inability to start something. If you're bored, the trick is to start something. This can be anything, for example taking the rubbish out. This will lead to the shed, which will in turn lead to some low-level pottering, which will finally lead to a lifetime of absorption in the construction of a scale model of a llama made from rusty nails and then, quite possibly, the Turner Prize.

How to Feel Guilty

You're right to feel guilty. You know you shouldn't have done it. Bend over. This is a rough summary of the derivation of the immense power of the church and local traffic regulations. Let's just be thankful that traffic wardens don't also have a priestly function.

The Guilty Party is the political wing of the church. It works on the basis that everyone is guilty until proven innocent. This state arose through the so-called original sin where Adam ate the apple from the tree of knowledge. These days Adam would be congratulated on a significant contribution to his five portions of fruit a day.

Guilt is a homesickness for a parallel universe where you are a much better person. It's a painful and persistent reminder that you could now be feeling virtuous if you hadn't just consumed the tub of ice cream, the contents of the petty-cash tin or the body of your best friend's partner.

The secret of living guilt-free is not to avoid doing anything bad as even the holiest of people are racked with guilt at the most minor of omissions. Instead, you should have no concept of good and bad and just do whatever you please. Foxes don't feel guilty about chickens.

One of the reasons court dramas are so popular is that they have a verdict at the end where someone is found innocent or guilty. In the real world nothing is so clean cut; things are naughty but nice, innocent but wicked, or bad but understandable. Only the last judgement will sort everything out, unless you feel your human rights have been breached.

There are two kinds of guilt. The first is not doing what you've been told to do, which is bearable. The second is not doing what you personally know you should have done, which is not. Guilt is incredibly tenacious in the memory, possibly to stop you doing the same bad thing twice. The memory of pleasure is much weaker, unless of course it's a guilty pleasure.

The guilt problem has given rise to the brilliant idea of a scapegoat: an entirely innocent party, normally a goat or someone not present at a committee meeting, who takes the blame for the sins of the group. That's why you should never miss a committee meeting and why goat's cheese tastes slightly odd.

How to Self-Help

S elf-help is emotional DIY and the self-help section in bookshops is the equivalent of B&Q. In the old days, personal growth used to mean a wart. Now it means something far more unpleasant. Self-help is a bit of a misnomer because it generally requires the help of a guru in book form. People who buy self-help books are always nice people. You won't find total bastards picking up a copy of *Unleash the Pleasant Person Within*.

Self-help books vary in quality. If you find yourself drilling a hole in your head to let the demons out, it's probably best to take that one back to the library. It's a shame that there isn't a monthly self-help magazine which you could collect and keep in a special binder until you had a complete personality.

Often people with the same kind of problem like to join self-help groups. Be wary if your group offers life membership as clearing up your problem fast is unlikely to be a priority. Self-help is addictive and you can spend so much time with yourself up on blocks that you don't actually get out any more.

Some people enjoy self-help so much they get someone to do it for them. These people are called therapists and are paid to find everything you say interesting. The difference between a therapist and a friend is that the friend won't ask you to lie down before talking. If they do, they might be about to stretch the limits of friendship.

Most self-help books work by identifying a failing you have and then curing it for you. There could be a book called *Count Your Blessings and Pull Yourself Together* but it would be very thin and would have to be padded out with a Ten-Step Counting/Pulling Programme.

All self-help books promise a significantly nicer and more powerful you underneath the normal pathetic you. Be warned, though, if you manage to release the fearless smiling extrovert within, it's very difficult to put it back. Also remember that most self-help books are written by Americans and you might inadvertently release your inner American.

British self-help books tend to fall at the first hurdle. There would need to be an introductory volume called *First Take Yourself Seriously*. Many people prefer liquid self-improvement, where the effect is more immediate and you don't have to listen to accompanying CDs. Finally, don't confuse self-help with helping yourself. One will lead to inner peace, the other to a conviction for shoplifting.

How to be Instinctive

The MP3 player is the enemy of instinct. It's very difficult to feel a subtle tingling in your spine when you have a heavy bass line being pumped directly into your cerebral cortex. Instinct can only make itself heard in silence, which is why it's almost completely unnoticed and unused in the modern world.

Instinct acts as a kind of behavioural satnav. It's a quiet and reassuring inner voice that will always give you guidance if you can be bothered to tune into it. However, humans are always suspicious of inner voices, especially if there's more than one of them.

Instinct is all the accumulated wisdom of a thousand generations of human beings hard-wired into our little heads. Sadly this is then very quickly obscured by the formal process of education. Instinct is a mixture of the common sense that tells you when something supposedly good is actually a load of cobblers and also of the uncommon sense that warns you of things that normally come without warning.

Seeing things with your own eyes is generally held to be a good way of verifying things. But eyes are screens and like any screen they don't tell the whole story. Getting a feel for things is much more effective as it lets your sixth sense have a sniff round. As a French philosopher once said, instinct is the nose of the mind. It sounds slightly odd, but instinctively you know it's right.

Don't confuse listening to your instinct with being yourself. If you listen very closely, your instinct is often telling you to be somebody quite different. And that's generally the point where people stop listening to their instinct and plug their earphones back in.

How to be Optimistic

Optimists think that not only is the glass half full but it's a lovely glass and someone will be along in a moment to top it up. A few people are neither optimists nor pessimists and for them the glass is simply twice as big as it needs to be. The glass-half-empty attitude is alarmingly prevalent. For instance, you never hear people being happy that reservoirs are half full; or that the surface of the earth is one third dry land; or that almost two thirds of marriages are happy.

Pessimists are people born in a minor key. They generally like to think they're realists moulded from bitter experience. Optimists, meanwhile, don't have bitter experiences. On the contrary, losing that leg/job/lottery ticket was the best possible thing that could have happened to them. Indeed, there are some pathological optimists around, emotional corks who have incredible internal buoyancy.

Optimists are always thinking that things could be a lot worse, which means that they actually have a very acute sense of pessimism. Similarly, pessimists are closet optimists in that they continually have a vision of how much better things could be if they weren't quite so bad.

Both optimism and pessimism are self-fulfilling prophecies, which is either great or disastrous news depending on what you are in the first place. Pessimists are born, not made, and have no hope of becoming optimists, which can't help matters. Optimists know that pessimists will always be miserable, which itself is a cheery thought.

Some trades are prone to pessimism. The media, for example, is the mouthpiece of pessimism because if no news is good news, then all news is bad news. Engineering is full of optimism in that you can't stay in the business without a strong belief that things are going to go up and stay up.

If optimism is helium of the personality, then bornagain Christians are little balloons of optimism where somebody has let go of the string. The dark side of optimism is that people with a sunny personality can begin to think that the sun is actually shining from a part of their anatomy. They are so bright and shiny that everyone nearby is thrown into a darker shadow. Of course there must also be a bright side to pessimism. But no one's ever going to find it.

How to be Content

Contentment is nature's Prozac. It keeps you going through the bad times and the good without making too much fuss of either. Happiness is a fine marmalade but contentment is a citrus grove. Children are naturally content because they don't know any different. It's the knowledge of difference that breeds discontent and it's when you finally realize that difference makes no difference that you can reclaim contentment.

It may sound dull, but being content is a profoundly radical position. It means you have no outstanding needs that other people, events or corporations can satisfy. You can't be manipulated, corrupted, conned, heartbroken or sold unnecessary insurance policies. Contentment is the real peace of mind – the peace of mind that insurance policies always claim to sell. Its definition varies between people but generally includes someone to love, somewhere to live and something to eat. And, almost always, one item of sentimental value.

The path to contentment is well signposted but generally points in the opposite direction to where we want to travel. Instead we rush off getting everything we want and then realize we don't need any of it. A quicker way to contentment is to realize you don't need any of the things you think you want before spending forty years trying to acquire them.

Being happy with your lot seems to be the essence of contentment. If you have been chosen to be one of life's good-looking millionaires, you just have to accept your fate and not continually struggle against it. Being unhappy with your lot is perfectly understandable when the one you've been given is absolute rubbish. Sadly there is no cosmic car boot sale where you can get rid of the lot you're not happy with. All you can do is look at other people's car boots and be happy with the junk you've got in your own.

Restless discontent is often held up as the great well-spring of personal and artistic progress. This is the ants-in-the-pants theory of progress and works well if you think progress consists of substituting one state of unhappiness with another. That said, contentment can be dangerously close to the squishy sofas of smugness and complacency. It's worth remembering your lot can quite easily be an epic struggle against overwhelming odds but, even if it is, you can still be content with it.

How to Know Yourself

A lot of very big thinkers have concluded that knowing yourself is a very good thing to do. This doesn't mean that it's a good thing for everyone else to know you too and that you should hold big parties to help more people do this. What it means is that a greater understanding of yourself will help you in life.

It's actually a lot easier to study the great thinkers who said you should know yourself than it is to go to the effort of actually knowing yourself. There are no study guides to oneself, although hearing what your ex-partners say behind your back can be useful in this regard.

Getting to know yourself is a rigorous and unsparing examination of all your many strengths and one or two minor weaknesses. However, it can come as a bit of a shock to get to know yourself and find that you're really not the sort of person you want to know at all.

On average, for every year of life you have, it takes about two years to understand exactly what happened. Most people never catch up and therefore die confused.

That's why hermits sit on top of mountains: they are cutting down their input of experiences so that their understanding can catch up.

Some people prefer reinventing themselves to knowing themselves. These are the kind of people who learn Spanish one week and Karate the next. Sadly, they're putting more experience in their personal compost than they will ever be able to spread on the gooseberries of enlightenment.

The best way to get to know yourself is to get to know other people. They will teach you about yourself faster than you can on your own. Enemies and in-laws are the best for this as neither have anything to lose in telling you the complete and unvarnished truth.

The danger of knowing yourself and knowing other people is that you become a know-all. What you really need to do is to unknow yourself and unlearn everything you've learned. Once you've done this, you realize one of three things: there is a God, there isn't a God, or you are God, depending on your innate sense of self-importance.

Getting to know oneself is like a coconut: on the outside there is a big squashy green layer that helps us rub along in life; then there is the hard inner brown shell which is the protective layer that ensures our survival; underneath that is the soft flesh that only our loved ones penetrate; finally and right inside is the coconut milk. No one knows what this is for as coconuts don't suckle their young. At the heart of everyone is a great mystery.

How to Go with the Flow

Humans are made up of 70 per cent water and, like any other body of water, we feel a deep urge to make our way to the seaside. That's why holidays by the sea are so popular, because at a molecular level it's like going home.

In the river of life some people think they're in charge and move forward through a complex series of canals and locks; these are the control freaks in their narrow boats. Others relax in their canoes, occasionally encountering a bit of white water, but generally just drifting happily along. Some people have paddles and try to steer things a little but others don't have a paddle at all and occasionally find themselves in unsuitable creeks.

Before you decide to go with the flow, it's always best to check where the flow is coming from. In the countryside you shouldn't drink from a stream if there's a chance that there's a dead sheep in it slightly further up. In the same way it's always worth checking exactly where new jobs and new partners spring from.

To really go with the flow, it helps if you don't care where you're going. Only the very rich or the very poor can pull this one off: the rich because they create their own flow, the poor because they don't have a boat. The flow most people are going with is called the rat race. This is a very powerful current of work and family that carries most people down the storm drain of their lives, washing them out on the beach of old age before they've even admired the view.

A few people choose to swim against the tide. There are three possible consequences of doing this: you become a very powerful swimmer but don't get anywhere; you escape the tide and find new rock pools of happiness; you drown.

Whether you go with it or not, the flow always continues because the passage of life is ever onward. This is worth knowing because sometimes stepping out of the flow for a while allows it to bring you things from further upstream. Meditation is an attempt to mentally step outside the flow of life and find stillness. A glass of wine, on the other hand, creates a pleasurable internal flow that makes the less pleasant external flow easier to manage.

How to Live

People who are about to die generally don't regret the parachute jumps they haven't made (unless they're falling from an aircraft without one). Instead they regret the love they haven't given or haven't expressed. Generally the reason they haven't done this is because they've been too full of hate, too in love with themselves or simply too crushed by the business of survival.

The universe is in balance. If it wasn't, it wouldn't exist. Every constituent part of the universe is also in balance, including us. Life therefore is a question of balance. On the tightrope of life, the pole we have to balance with always has two sides: light and dark, male and female, good and bad. Acknowledging and understanding both sides is the only way of keeping upright and moving forward.

To get through life requires effort and luck. Generally the harder you try, the luckier you get, but not always. Sometimes superhuman effort fails and, at other times, absolutely minimal effort succeeds spectacularly. That said, try trying first. Everyone has free will in life but what happens to you is largely out of your control. We're like fleas on the head of an ox: we may be jumping around merrily but the overall direction of travel is not really in our hands.

The secret of life is a combination of the accumulated wisdom of the great thinkers down the ages and the Cub Scout law: be nice to other people and do your best. It doesn't sound very inspiring but, on balance, it's probably right. Remember, too, that there's a reason that the universe is in balance. We don't know what it is but it's likely to be a lot more impressive than we are.